Everyday Faith

*Finding the God of Eternity
in the Everyday of Life*

R.G. Glover

Everyday Faith
Copyright © 2023 R.G. Glover
All rights reserved.

No part of this publication may be reproduced in any form or by any electronic or mechanical means, including information storage and retrieval systems, without permission in writing by the publisher or author, except by a reviewer who may quote brief passages in a review.

Scripture taken from the Modern English Version. Copyright © 2014 by Military Bible Association. Used by permission. All rights reserved.

Cover Design: Elizabeth Little, Hyliian Graphics
Cover images: ©R.G. Glover
Publishing assistant: The Author's Mentor,
www.TheAuthorsMentor.com

ISBN-13: 9798676619961
Also in available eBook format
V10312023SC

PUBLISHED IN THE UNITED STATES OF AMERICA

Dedication

I would like to dedicate this work to all those wonderful Christians who have prayed for me and encouraged me throughout my life. I know that prayer works, and I believe that miracles still happen.

To the One to whom all those prayers are directed, I dedicate this book and all that I do to You and Your Son. I pray that You would bless the words found on these pages and anyone who takes the time to read them.

Table of Contents

Introduction 1
How Deep Is Your Faith? 5
Put Down The Bottle 8
House Cleaning 10
How The Story Ends 12
Warning, Consumption Of This Product May 14
Faith Like Gracie 17
The New Washing Machine 19
Knowing The Real 21
Backward Napkins 23
Ear Candy 25
The Kitchen 28
Lyra's Joy 30
Our Promised Future 32
Not What I Expected 34
Spoiler Alert 36
The Flattery Of Imitation 38
I Forgive . . . Me 40
Being All In 42
Here, Let Me Explain 44
Cancelled 46
Following Your Shadow 48

One Day At A Time	50
Sticks And Stones	52
Your Thought Cup	54
Keep It Simple	56
Daring To Submit	58
Created To Be	60
Knowing The Cost	62
One More	65
Ever Increasing	67
The Other R.	69
Wishing You Can	72
Speaking The Same Language	74
A.K.A., A Man Of God	76
Cat Skinnin'	79
On Target	81
Your Filter	84
Overcoming Mountains	86
A One-Size God	88
One Single Degree	90
Non-Smudging Ink	93
The Master Manipulator	95
God Has Your Back	98
Being Unknown	100
Just The Minimum	102
The Missing Piece	104
Your Storehouse	106
Loving The Unseen	108
The Next Time	110

Once In A Lifetime	112
The Moon Is Always Full	115
Again	117
The Lost Circle Walk	119
Why Not?	121
The Transfer	123
Only One Mudhole	126
Craving Oxygen	128
A Work In Progress	130
The "Perfect" Worship Service	132
Out With The Old	134
Change Is A Two-Way Request	136
The Gracious Servant	138
Footprints On The Moon	140
Being In Sync	142
The Specialist	144
Pass It On	146
The End Of The Rope	148
Moderation	150
Closer Than Appearances	152
Knowing The Tree	155
The Smallest Battlefield	157
Spiritual Exercise	159
Two Types Of People	161
Roots And All	163
Getting Into Practice	165
A Face For Radio	167
End Of Sentence	169

I Don't Believe You! 171
The Crowd You Run With 173
Your Safety Net 175
Off On A Good Note... 177
Spinners.. 179
B U T... 181
At Least I'm Not 184
Foundation Or Façade?.. 186
Pruning For Effect.. 188
The Squeaky Wheel 190
Why Work?.. 192
A First Place Christian 194
Chicken Or A Pig?.. 196
If It Ain't Broke 199
Behind Enemy Lines... 201
Why Follow God?.. 203
Being Contagious 205
Knowing About God... 207
Who, Or What, Is "It"? 209
Full Of Good News 211
I'm Telling You, Something's Not Right 213
Why Pick Judas?.. 216
Bandwagon Jumpers 218
The Boss Is Looking 221
How Many Times?.. 223
There's No Way 225
Perishable Things.. 227
Washing Dishes 229

Belief In A Sign	231
Looking Forward To It	233
Salvation Is Not . .	235
Watch Your Step	237
Things That Last	239
My Delete Key	241
One Gate	243
Until Next Time	245
Just One Thing	248
Wanting What I Have	250
Plan B	253
No App For That	256
Exactly Like Me	258
God's Fruit Basket	260
A Day To Celebrate	262
Limited Expectations	264
Leave That Alone!	266
Acknowledgments	269
Author's Bio	271

And without faith it is impossible to please God, for he who comes to God must believe that He exists and that He is a rewarder of those who diligently seek Him. (Hebrews 11:6)

INTRODUCTION

Wow. Book 2? Can you believe it? I actually wrote a Book 1 and now there's a Book 2? And to think that . . . Whoa, I'm beginning to sound like Dr. Seuss. First, allow me to thank you, kind reader. Hopefully, the collection you now hold will give you a few hours of pleasure. Having said that, if, after you have read the final word of the final story and closed the book, a bit of pleasure is the only thing you have received, in one respect, I have failed you. One of my goals in sharing these stories is not only to bring a potential smile, but also to lead you to reflect on your life and the eternal God who took the time to create both you and me. As I write these stories, I often look back and remember the things and the people God has placed in my path, ultimately leading me, now more than sixty-years old, to sit in this chair, staring at a computer screen while typing on this keyboard. I know one thing: had I been steering the ship, my life wouldn't have led me to this chair in this room typing these words.

Perhaps you are wondering why I would begin this introduction with the words "Book 2." I suppose I could have started it *The Book of Second Randy* but that sounds a little pretentious. Anyway, being the second in a series of faith-based story collections, to me, Book 2 seemed the logical beginning. If you were one of the millions (okay, perhaps millions is a slight – well big – exaggeration) who read *A Leap Of Faith*, my first collection of stories, AND you have picked up *Everyday Faith*, thank you. I hope there was something in *A Leap Of Faith* that made you take a moment or two to jot down a few thoughts or memories.

Sometime after finishing *A Leap Of Faith*, I was asked how I expected someone to read the book. After resisting the temptation to sarcastically answer, "One word at a time," I asked the questioner for clarification. "What do you mean?"

"Well, is this a daily devotional? Is there a particular pattern I should follow? Do I read a story then wait a few days then read another? Do I read the entire thing in order or should I skip around?"

Having read several daily devotional books, I understood the questions. More than most, I understand that we want structure in our lives. Structure leads to order and order often leads to progress. So I answered, "I'm not sure. You can read any story you want whenever you think the time is right. You can read *Happy December 25th* around Christmas and you can read *What's Not To Love?* around Valentine's Day, or you can read them whenever you are led to do so." So I will address these questions of how to read these stories.

Everyday Faith, as with *A Leap Of Faith*, can be read in any order you wish. The stories aren't grouped in any particular order. A story's title may lead you to think it should be read during a certain time. *The Moon Is Always Full* not only applies to a full moon but to any and all stages of our nearest heavenly body. Perhaps, after reading that story, you will look at the moon and see it in a different light.

Some readers also pointed out to me that my devotions aren't typical devotions. I'll agree; my stories aren't typical devotions. The "typical" devotional book will have stories limited to somewhere around 300 words, often fewer, and those stories are grouped around some sort of theme (e.g., Devotions for High School Graduates, Devotions for New Parents, Devotions for the Outdoorsman, etc.). Because my stories are a touch longer (averaging a little over 550 words), a friend described them as sort of mini-essays (emphasis on mini). Why would I not write typical devotions? Two reasons. One: Over the years, I have come to believe that most of us are anything but typical. One reason we should never judge is because we never know what someone is going through at any particular moment in time. The only typical thing about typical is how it is spelled and for some, even that is not the case. Two: Call me crazy, but I believe God gave me the stories found within these pages. If God wants me to use more than 300 words to write a story, who am I to reason with Him and tell Him the world has defined limitations. Moses tried that "reasoning with God" thing and he still led the Hebrew people out of Egypt. God is not a God of limitations and I am not going to start limiting Him (hence the story *Limited Expectations*).

"But Randy," you may say, "I believe we are typical because we all have things in common." That is true, especially for a Christian. As New Testament, born-again, Christians, there are certain beliefs we must share. We believe that God the Father, God the Son, and God the Spirit make up the Holy Trinity. We know that Jesus was born in Bethlehem from a virgin mother. We know He lived a sinless life and He died on a cross because of our sins. We know on the third day after His death, He rose from the tomb. We know everyone sins and that only through the blood of Jesus can we be saved from those sins. We know we must receive that gift of salvation to enter our promised heavenly home. We know once we are saved by grace through faith, we are always saved and our sins (past, present, AND future) will never be counted against us. Those are, no, those must be the beliefs of the "typical" Christian.

But I also know we are all different. Other than salvation, we all have different reasons for needing God at different times in our lives. I don't write typical devotions because we, and the problems we have, aren't typical. While all of us committed our sins against the same God and all of us who are Christians received forgiveness of our sins from that same God, none of us has committed the exact same sins. My hope is that these "non-typical" stories might offer help in various times throughout your life. There is no right or wrong order to these stories. All of us have daily issues. Two weeks ago, *One More* was just 573 words on paper; today, it may be the exact 573 words you may need.

While we may not be typical, I know I will always need a most untypical God in my most typical of ways. God is my Father and Savoir, He is my redeemer and provider and sustainer. He is my light in the darkness. He is my eternal everything. Above all else, He is my one and only God.

Thank you, again for picking up this book. I hope you enjoy the stories. And for whatever you may be going through, just like you will find in the story *Overcoming Mountains*, I pray that God will lead you to the other side of the valley of your problems and to the mountaintop that awaits you.

Happy reading,
Randy

Eternal God. I Thank You for the gift that is Your story. Amen.

> *When He entered the house, the blind men came to Him. And Jesus said to them, "Do you believe that I am able to do this?" They said to Him, "Yes, Lord." Then He touched their eyes, saying, "According to your faith, let it be done for you."*
> (Matthew 9:28-29)

HOW DEEP IS YOUR FAITH?

How many times have I asked God for help? How about I start by telling you about the night I had to walk five miles to the house because I did something stupid. Again. How many times? Too many times to count. When we ask God for His help, how much help do we truly, from the bottom of our heart, expect He will provide? All too often, we ask for something in prayer that, if we are being honest, we don't expect a 100% answer.

A few months ago, I was sleeping like the proverbial baby until about 2:30 a.m. when I was rudely awakened by something so small that unless it wanted to be noticed, many of us would never notice it. At first glance, four millimeters doesn't seem like a big thing, especially when you learn that four millimeters is a little less than a quarter of an inch. But when you learn that the four-millimeter intruder is none other than a kidney stone that could play a sand spur's stunt double, four millimeters tends to get your attention.

I tried to wait it out but, as they usually do, the kidney stone won, so I dressed myself and got into my vehicle, intent on driving myself to the emergency room. However, after four miles (about half-way), I had to pull over. The pain was nearing the, "I'm about to pass out" level. I parked my vehicle, got out, and squatted beside the door, pleading that God would DO SOMETHING AND DO IT RIGHT NOW! After about thirty seconds, the pain subsided and I was able to continue my trip. Wonder of wonders, every traffic light on my way to the hospital was green. Believe it or not, the emergency room was hardly busy and I was able to be diagnosed, have a cat scan, and receive some much-needed chemical relief within 20 minutes. Did God have anything to do with my speedy treatment? I choose to believe He did. God did something, and He did it right then.

Think about this: if we were the two blind men from the opening verse, how much better would we be able to see? Jesus told them they would be able to see because they believed He could heal them. As they were blind, it's obvious that they hadn't seen Jesus heal anyone, but they believed what their hearts told them was possible. When we constantly approach the throne of heaven with half-hearted requests, is it any wonder we only receive half blessings? The following passages from the Modern English Version of the Bible are just a few examples that remind us that our requests should be filled with the faith of the blind men:

- Matthew 9:22 – Jesus to the sick woman – "Your faith has made you well."
- Matthew 21:22 – Jesus to His disciples – "And whatever you ask in prayer, if you believe, you will receive."
- Mark 10:52 – Jesus to blind Bartimaeus – "Go your way. Your faith has made you well."
- James 1:6 – "But let him ask in faith, without wavering. For he who wavers is like a wave of the sea, driven and tossed with the wind."

Peter showed us an example of deep faith as he stepped from the relative safety of a small boat in a storm-tossed sea so he could walk – ON WATER – to his Lord and friend, Jesus. As much as I would want the faith that Peter exhibited when he released the boat, I find myself being like the other disciples in the storm, huddled in the false security the boat seemed to provide. I don't need the faith of the sighted; I need the faith of the blind.

The depth of our faith has nothing to do with the depth of our problems. The depth of our faith is what allows us to walk across our sea of problems to the One who can get us through what ever problems we have.

*Lord Jesus. Instead of the elephant-sized doubt that Satan is
quick to give, I ask that You grant me the faith of the tiny
mustard seed. I have a few mountains
I need to move. Amen.*

> *Everyone who lives on milk is unskilled in the word of righteousness, for he is a baby. But solid food belongs to those who are mature, for those who through practice have powers of discernment that are trained to distinguish good from evil.*
> (Hebrews 5:13-14)

PUT DOWN THE BOTTLE

Babies. Of all the gifts God gives us, babies have to be one of the top three. A baby comes into the world totally helpless. The first thing a baby feeds on is its mother's milk. And for a while, that milk is all the baby needs. That milk meets all of the baby's nutritional requirements. After a while, the milk must be supplemented with other food so the baby progresses from milk to runny cereal, which is somewhat solid but not quite. As the baby grows, vegetables, fruits, and breads are added to the menu. Eventually, even these don't quite provide every essential element, so the baby takes the last step and meat is introduced to the baby's palate.

For an adult, a well-rounded diet includes all of the food groups. If milk were the only requirement of an adult diet, why would God grant Adam the permission to eat other things? Later in the Bible, God told Peter that he could eat all things, not just the foods that Peter had been told were "clean."

For a Christian, Genesis 1:1 and John 3:16 are the spiritual equivalent of biblical milk. When someone first becomes a Christian, there is a good chance they have already received some spiritual milk. They believe Jesus is who He says He is and they also believe the ABCs of how to become a Christian. Believing in the death of Jesus because of our sins, His burial in a tomb, and His subsequent resurrection from that tomb are spiritual milk. Just like a baby needs some solid food, the Christian must, in order to grow their spiritual life, eventually move from the kiddie table to the adult table and consume some solid spiritual food.

Recognizing God's work in our daily life is spiritual food. A consistent prayer life is spiritual food. Daily Bible reading is fine, but reading the Bible just to say you are reading the Bible is the equivalent of spiritual formula; Bible study is spiritual food. Witnessing, serving, leading a prayer group, and teaching a Sunday school class – those and other things are the "meat and potatoes" of the Christian life.

Mother's milk is fine for the infant baby. Spiritual milk is fine for the new Christian. If we want to graduate from new Christian to adult Christian, we must put aside our spiritual bottles, pick up our spiritual knife, fork, and spoon, find a seat at the adult table, and begin taking in the solid food that God wants us to eat. Supper's ready, let's start eating.

Father God. Thank You for the spiritual milk You give us when we are baby Christians. I pray that You would give each of us a craving for some good, old-fashioned, solid Christian food.
Amen.

What? Do you not know that your body is the temple of the Holy Spirit, who is in you, whom you have received from God, and that you are not your own? You were bought with a price. Therefore glorify God in your body and in your spirit, which are God's. (1 Corinthians 6:19-20)

HOUSE CLEANING

Cleaning house, spring cleaning, throwing stuff out, or, "Hurry! Company's coming! This place is a mess!" No matter how you say it, from time-to-time, most of us need to do a thorough house cleaning. Those trinkets need dusting, the baseboards need cleaning, tubs and toilets need scrubbing, floors need mopping, carpets need cleaning, and maybe the walls could stand a new coat of paint. To whatever degree, every now and then, our houses all need a good cleaning.

When I bought my house, my kitchen cabinets, being only three years old, were sparkling white. Now that my house is nearing fifteen years old, I can tell the cabinets aren't quite as white as they once were. I look at my walls and I think, "How did that spot get there?" How about when you go to a restaurant? Do you want to eat on a table that feels less than clean? There is a particular pizza place I really like. Whenever I go there and am waiting in line, I find myself running my finger along the shelves, wondering how much dust has collected there. I'd rather not say the name of the place, but the pizza is good.

The Bible tells me that when someone becomes a Christian, their body no longer belongs to them. God sends His Holy Spirit to live within that person. But before the Holy Spirit can move in, God must clean that house so it will be fit for His Spirit. If we look at our lives, are we satisfied that we have done our best to keep the house of God's Spirit as clean as we can? Would our life and the way we talk and the things we do pass a white glove inspection?

Yes, I know I'm a Christian, I know that my sins have been forgiven, and I know that my name is written in God's heavenly reservation book, but are there things in my life that need to be thrown to the curb? Does my "secret" life truly reflect my beliefs? If we look deeply enough, most of us will find a bad habit or two that needs to be cleaned out.

Since houses don't clean themselves, I find that I have to put forth some effort to keep mine livable. The same goes for my spiritual house. Now that I think about it, I need to put down the mouse and pick up my broom.

Lord God. Thank You for cleaning my spiritual house so Your Holy Spirit could move in. Remind me that I need to clean my life of the things that cause sinful clutter so my house will remain as clean as can be. Amen.

> *And I heard a loud voice from heaven, saying, "Look! The tabernacle of God is with men, and He will dwell with them. They shall be His people, and God Himself will be with them and be their God. God shall wipe away all tears from their eyes. There shall be no more death. Neither shall there be any more sorrow nor crying nor pain, for the former things have passed away.* (Revelation 21:3-4)

HOW THE STORY ENDS

Some have asked me why I enjoy writing. Of the many answers I could give, the simplest one would be that I enjoy writing because I first enjoyed reading. For as long as I can remember, I have found a certain degree of satisfaction in the world of imagination that is a good book. Although my favorite book – the Bible – is a work of non-fiction, I truly enjoy well-written fiction. Any author who can, through dialog and description, when accompanied by my imagination, take me to a world that exists only on paper, has a God-given gift.

When I was younger, I would intentionally open the book to the last page and read the last sentence before beginning the story. Like many people, I was curious about the ending of the story. I no longer begin at the end, but if I'm reading a particularly good book, the ten-year-old boy that still lives within me sometimes surfaces and wants to take a peek ahead to find out what happens to the main character.

As someone who has read the entire Bible, front-to-back, more than a few times, I can tell you how the story ends. If you are a Christian and you've read the same story, you should find that ending refreshing. If you don't know how the story ends, I'll give you a hint: our side wins. I hope I didn't spoil it for you, but, in the end, God and Christ reign victorious over Lucifer and his schemes.

As reassuring as it is to know what happens in the end, it can also be heartbreaking. The same Bible that tells us God does not want any to perish but wants all to come to repentance (2 Peter 3:9b) also tells us that there are those who will not believe and will be condemned (Mark 16:16). We, as those saved by Christ, should also want, more than anything else, all to come to the saving knowledge that is the Good News of the Gospel.

God was there in the beginning. God is here in the middle. And God will be with us, as Jesus says in the final verse of Matthew, 'til the end of the age. We win. Now it's up to us to tell all we know how they, too, can be on the winning side.

Christ Jesus. Thank You for the Bible that tells us what will happen in the end. I pray, Lord, that all would come to the saving knowledge that is Your gift of eternal salvation. Amen.

> *Then Death and Hades were cast into the lake of fire. This is the second death. Anyone whose name was not found written in the Book of Life was cast into the lake of fire.*
> *Revelation 20:14-15*

WARNING, CONSUMPTION OF THIS PRODUCT MAY...

Okay, by show of hands, how many of you believe that cigarette smoking could potentially be a bad thing? Very good, you can put your hands down; you're reading a book. Next question, how about smokeless tobacco? What about excessive consumption of alcohol or ultra-sugary soft drinks or swallowing large amounts of fatty fried foods or made-from-scratch cheesecake? What makes us believe those things are bad for our health? Need a hint? Okay.

If you look on the side of a pack of cigarettes or other tobacco product, you will find a warning that was issued by the Surgeon General of the United States, a doctor very few people know, but a lot of people try to follow his advice. That warning tells us that consumption of certain products, including those containing tobacco, have the potential to cause adverse health effects. We can also find warnings about eating too much processed sugar and white flour, failure to wear a seatbelt, running with scissors, crossing the street without looking, or jumping from bridges just because our friends did. You name the activity and there's a chance that, sometime in our lives, we were warned against doing that particular thing. Would you believe there's a warning against drinking too much water? There is, look it up.

I'm not a betting man, but I'll wager there are some of you who actually pay attention to those warnings. Why? Because someone with an assumed level of authority, acquired by either education or experience, told you there was a potential danger associated with the product or the activity. Even if you experimented, you eventually saw the light and came to your senses. Suppose the Bible had a warning label.

If the Bible had a warning label, it might say something like this: "Warning, failure to follow the words found in these pages has been proven to lead to a lifetime of poor decision making followed by an eternity of pain and suffering." Do you think that would convince some to take the time to read about God's love for us? Maybe. I fear some would continue to live as they are living, going through life with no thought of the potential – yet promised – consequences.

For years, the Surgeon General has warned people about the dangers of smoking, myself included. Even though it's been more than twenty-five years since my last cigarette, from the time I was fifteen until I turned thirty-four, I smoked thousands of them. Although some people ignore the warnings and pay the price, others – including me – ignored the warnings and, as far as we know, suffered no ill effects. If only the negative effects of smoking and other vices were immediately apparent, I would imagine I, and millions of others, would have never taken that first drag.

It's true, not all warnings about the hazards of earthly vices come to pass. But that warning about failing to follow the words found in the Bible, if you continue to ignore it, I can guarantee you there is an ultimate and eternal price you will pay.

Father God. I pray that everyone would heed the words found in Your Word, the Bible. I pray that the warnings You give us about this life and the potential life that awaits us would be taken to heart so those hearts can be given to You. Amen.

R.G. Glover

So that your faith should not stand in the wisdom of men, but in the power of God. (1 Corinthians 2:5)

FAITH LIKE GRACIE

Ahh, Gracie. Her faith is like . . . Who, you may be wondering, is Gracie? And while I'm at it, what does her faith have to do with anything? Fair enough. The aforementioned Gracie is a member of my family. She's about eight inches tall and about eighteen inches long, if you include her ever-wagging tail. Gracie, a Chihuahua, is one of my two dogs, the other being Sunny, a terrier mix.

I adopted Sunny on a cold January morning in 2012. A few months later, I thought she might like a "sister" to keep her occupied while I was away during the day. Back to the Shelby County Humane Society I went, looking for a similar sized dog. After looking at the choices, I couldn't find anything that was close to the size of Sunny (she weighs 16 pounds). After being directed to the small dog room, I saw this little, nearly white Chihuahua with a look of perpetual worry on her face. She seemed sweet, so she joined my household.

Gracie, you might say, is an industrial strength lap dog. I sit down and she jumps to my lap; I'm guessing she thinks my lap is her lap. She's extremely content until she hears any sudden or loud noise. A clap of thunder or the shot of a firework and she burrows in, knowing I will protect her from whatever is making that awful sound. If I'm standing and she hears one of those noises, she will put her feet on my leg with the "pick me up and protect me" look on her little face. As soon as I bend over and pick her up, she begins to nervously whimper while she wraps her front feet around my arm. The whimpering will cease, but only when the noise stops and her feet touch the floor is she fully at ease, at least as "at ease" as a nervous Chihuahua can be. You see, Gracie wants to be picked up until she *is* picked up. Then she immediately wants to be put down.

We Christians are sometimes like Gracie. We ask God what we can do to serve Him; then, when He answers, we immediately start wondering how in the world we are going to do whatever it is He has called us to do. We tell God that we want to fly, but we don't want to fly too high. As soon as we get out of our comfort zone, we begin wondering how long it will be before we feel our feet touch familiar ground. We forget who is holding us up and we start focusing on how far we will fall when, not if, we fail. We tend to see the "why we can't" instead of "why we can," with God's help.

When Gracie gets scared, she comes running to me. When we need God's help, we call out to Him. If we ask God to pick us up, we needn't worry about how high we are; we just need to remember whose hands hold us.

Father God. I know I come to You with my share of problems and You have always helped me through them. God, remind me to focus not on how high You have to lift me to get over my mountains but to focus on the landing on the other side. Amen.

> *But we all are as an unclean thing, and all our righteousness is as filthy rags.* (Isaiah 64:6a)

THE NEW WASHING MACHINE

"Back in my day, when men were men." Sound familiar? Do you ever find yourself thinking that the things we use on a daily basis were once somehow . . . better? Some modern technology may tell you that you have a problem when you really don't, but most technology upgrades do tend to offer a fix that needed fixing. Take clothing. At one time, to have a shirt that had no wrinkles meant the shirt had to be starched and ironed with an iron that had been heated as it sat beside a fire. Now you can buy a shirt that promises to be wrinkle resistant, if not wrinkle-free. But clothes, regardless of their ability to resist wrinkles, get dirty, and dirty clothes must be washed. Which brings me to the humble washing machine.

There was a time that washing clothes meant taking them to the river and beating them against a good-sized rock. Time passed and some enterprising person came up with the idea of the washboard. Effort was still required, but that washboard was certainly better than that rock in both cleanliness and effort. Jump forward to 1782 and we find another invention, the first washing machine.

Although those first washing machines still required effort, as there was no external power source, somehow, this newfangled contraption was light years better than the rock at the river. Now let's leap forward to the 21st century. We have top loaders, front loaders, agitators, no agitators, better detergents, cleaning with steam, we've even found a way to clean with the power of oxygen. If the air can clean my clothes, why do I need a washing machine?

Throughout the years, mankind has striven to invent a machine that will remove all kinds of stains from our clothes. But it seems that no matter how hard we try, some stains simply refuse to be removed. Before we know it, those once-new clothes are relegated to the work pile or they find a new life as dirty rags.

Our lives are like that favorite white shirt. Before long, either because of being worn many times or because you ate food that shouldn't be eaten when wearing white, we notice that the shirt is no longer white. Regardless of the machine, the detergent, the pre-wash, the water temperature, or the wash cycle, that stubborn stain simply refuses to disappear. While the shirt may be forever ruined, our lives can be made to be as clean as new.

When we turn to Jesus and ask Him to remove the stain that is our sin, He does it. But we must remember that only Jesus can do that. No new religion, or new version of the Bible, or new church will remove those stains from our life. When we get tired of trying to clean ourselves up, we turn to Jesus.

In a few months, some company will introduce a new washing machine that promises to clean clothes better than ever. We don't need something new to clean our sins; that's been around since the beginning of time. Jesus was, is, and forever will be the perfect sin-cleaning machine.

My Lord and Savior. I thank You for the cleansing You provided for me and my life. Help me tell others that You are there for them when they get tired of trying. Amen.

> *But for us there is but one God, the Father, from whom are all things and for whom we exist. And there is one Lord Jesus Christ, through whom are all things and through whom we exist.* (1 Corinthians 8:6)

KNOWING THE REAL

In places that accept cash, pretty much anytime you present "folding money" to make a payment, that bill, be it a twenty, fifty, or a hundred, will undergo some amount of scrutiny in an effort to make sure it is not counterfeit. Why not ones, fives, and tens? There's not a lot of money in small bills, no pun intended. There are several ways to tell if a bill is the real thing. Some have a special strip embedded in the paper and some have a watermark that can be seen if held to light. You can even use a toothpick to identify a real one-hundred-dollar bill. Often the presented bill will be swiped with a marker containing special ink. If the money passes the test, the marker will show a specific color. Wrong color and you will probably find yourself explaining to the police where you got the money. No one likes counterfeit.

Just like counterfeit money, people can put forth an image claiming one thing when they are anything but that thing. We've all heard about someone trying to pawn themselves off as being ex-military or having some made-up ancestral heritage or pretending to be a doctor or attending some academic institution; you name the profession or the situation, someone has tried to fake their way through it. But, when it comes to eternity, counterfeit simply won't cut it.

Some have tried to convince others, with mixed degrees of success, that they are authentic Christians. They may play the part really well. To be honest, it's fairly easy to talk the talk of being a Christian. To fool some, you can simply go to church, carry a Bible, memorize a few scriptures, sing the songs, tell someone that you will be praying for them, and donate to charity. All of these look and sound good, but, when it comes to eternity, they fail the test.

You see, God has His marker ready to swipe the record of your life when you present yourself to Him. But God's marker doesn't change color if you're counterfeit; it doesn't leave a yellow or a black stripe. God's marker will check to see if the blood of Jesus covers your sin; no blood, no good.

Counterfeit money may fool some. In today's world, getting a fake ID, college degree, or work history is a fairly simple thing. You can pretend that you are a follower of Christ. But when God swipes your eternal soul, all the pretending in the world won't matter. God created us and He knows a true Christian when He sees one. The blood of Jesus is the only true mark of a Christian.

Eternal Father. I thank You for the perfect blood of Jesus. I know that it is only this blood that erases my sins and guarantees that my eternity is forever marked in Your book of life. Amen.

And whatever you do, do it heartily, as for the Lord and not for men. (Colossians 3:23)

BACKWARD NAPKINS

It seems like more and more restaurants are installing those 2-foot-tall napkin dispensers. And I guess I understand why they would want those things. They hold more napkins so less time is required to restock napkins. Most of them have a see-through cover so you will quickly know when the supply is running low. I appreciate the fact that I am the only person who touches the napkins I pull from the dispenser. Limit the number of people who touch the napkins and the chances of me catching something I didn't plan on catching are drastically reduced. But (isn't there always a but?), I do have one issue. Surprise!

Before I go on, let me say this is not specific to tall napkin dispensers because this bothered me years before those came into existence. I don't know if you know this, but napkins intended to be used with dispensers are folded a certain way. One side is solid napkin. The other side has a fold. This fold exists for two reasons: (1) it is intended to face outward and (2) it's supposed to align with the slot in the dispenser's cover, making it fairly easy to retrieve a single napkin when a single napkin is all that is needed. I wish I knew how many times I've opened napkin dispensers, removed the napkins from the dispenser, rearranged those napkins, and replaced them in the dispenser THE CORRECT WAY.

The Bible tells us that no matter what we do, we are to do it as if we are doing it for God. There are times we may ask if we can do something for the church. When we are told that someone is needed to help in the library or to pass out programs, we may see that as not enough of a challenge. The Gospel of Matthew tells us that we are to be responsible with what we are asked to do, no matter what it is. "His master said to him, 'Well done, you good and faithful servant. You have been faithful over a few things. I will make you ruler over many things. Enter the joy of your master'" (Matthew 25:21).

When we think a job is beneath us, are we tempted to do it half-heartedly? If so, remember that Satan is quick to point out any shortcoming we may have. Is stocking a napkin dispenser the most important job in the world? No. Is how we do our job a reflection of our belief in God? Most definitely. So, the next time you are tempted to half-heartedly do one of those jobs that you think no one notices, just remember this: the fold goes out. It really matters.

Eternal God. I know there are many things I am asked to do that pretty much anyone could do with no problem. Let me remember that whatever I do, I am to be grateful for the opportunity to help and I am to do it to the best of my ability. After all, I wouldn't have that ability if it weren't for You.
Amen.

And in their greed they will exploit you with deceptive words. Their judgment, made long ago, does not linger, and their destruction does not slumber. (2 Peter 2:3)

EAR CANDY

Okay, it's time to, as we say in the South, fess up. Who doesn't like some sort of candy? Be it caramel, peppermint, gum, chocolate, taffy, or licorice (if you can call that candy), whatever your favorite, most of us like some sort of sweet treat every now and again. I know I do. But I don't like all kinds of candy. I've already indicated licorice isn't on my list of go-to candy and neither is dark chocolate. However, add some peppermint to that dark chocolate and I'm in. I also like some brands of milk chocolate, especially when it's filled with gooey caramel goodness. But if you really want to make me happy, give me some of the white chocolate with peppermint candies you will find around Christmas time (note to candy makers, these are good year-round) and my candy enjoyment meter will be pegged.

There's one problem with candy. Too much of it does two things. One: it has the super ability to take away any desire for vegetables or fruit or stuff that's supposed to be good for you. While that may not seem like a bad idea at first, you really should eat some vegetables. I know that's candy blasphemy, but it's true. Number two: too much candy results in tooth decay. If you don't believe me, you can ask Dr. Stan, my dentist. He's one of them . . . how do you say it, experts. He's got a diploma and everything.

While the candy we eat can cause a hurting tummy or a toothache, the candy we hear can be much worse. When it comes to listening to spiritual flattery, also known as ear candy, those sweet, easy to hear, non-offensive words might sound good, but they rarely give us real spiritual nourishment. If all we ever hear is that God wants good things for us (which He does) or He just wants us to be happy (there's more to it than that), and maybe have the big house and the well-paying job, or having a beautiful wife or a handsome husband, ohhh, it's no wonder people think that's the God for them. How about those upbeat and uplifting songs of how happy life is for Christians and then we are told that all we have to do is feel good about ourselves. Talk about warm and fuzzies. Oooooo.

The truth is, if that's all you're getting from church, not only are you not being nourished, you are setting yourself up for some real spiritual decay. Ear candy, as nice as it may be, is not what your spiritual appetite needs. You may be full for a short time, but you'll soon be craving more candy. Just like any other drug, its satisfaction is short-lived. Then you come crawling back, needing yet another fix. Spiritual hunger doesn't need ear candy; it needs a real meat and potato and cornbread meal of Bible-based preaching.

If you can honestly say you've never felt that your preacher was talking directly to you, you've probably been getting a good dose of ear candy. If you skip all of those verses in the Bible that you don't like to read, you're hooked on ear candy. As much as Jesus talked about eternal salvation, He had many more warnings about eternal damnation. When it comes to satisfying our spiritual appetite, we need complete fulfillment. It's time we started eating our meat and vegetables and left the candy alone.

If you find yourself needing some spiritual food, put down the chocolate and pick up the knife and fork. Oh, and bring some napkins; spiritual meals can get a little messy.

Lord Jesus, steer me away from the easy words that can be found with ear candy. Sit me down at Your dinner table and feed me true spiritual nourishment until I am fully satisfied. Amen.

R.G. Glover

> *But a man may say, "You have faith and I have works." Show me your faith without your works, and I will show you my faith by my works.* (James 2:18)

THE KITCHEN

"If you can't stand the heat, get out of the kitchen!" The kitchen. The place where work is done and meals are made. All kitchens have tools: a stove, an oven, a refrigerator, sinks, mixers, knives, forks, spoons, bowls, and pans. I'm sure I've missed a few. As for the meals, all meals are prepared by someone reading a recipe that tells them the correct quantities of ingredients, the order of preparation, what temperature the oven must be set, and how much time is required to cook the dish. While all this may be true, a kitchen without a cook is pretty much worthless.

The cook is the person who drives the kitchen. Someone has to chop, mix, measure, and cook or no meal will be made. As for those dishes, utensils, pots, and pans, they don't wash and dry themselves. Kitchens are a place of activity, filled with hustle and bustle. Pretty much anyone can cook for one or two, but multiply that number by 100, or more, and you'll quickly find out who can cook and who can't.

Any worthwhile endeavor, be it cooking a meal, being a parent, or being a Christian, takes effort and dedication. There are going to be times when things come easy, and there will be times of testing. Just as being an effective teacher or cook requires dedication, preparation, experience, and some experimenting, being a Christian requires all of those things. Christians must pray, study God's Word, humble themselves, serve others, and sacrifice; and there are times it seems we must do many of these things simultaneously.

Almost anyone can make cheese toast or a bowl of oatmeal – at least the instant kind – but it takes a dedicated chef to make a soufflé or a quiche or a fancy dessert. Becoming a Christian gets you into heaven, but that's just the beginning. To be an effective Christian, we must be ready to step into God's kitchen and be prepared for the trial of fire that goes with being there. Don't hesitate, for God's Word tells us that this fire is what proves our Christian mettle. "Each one's work will be revealed. For the Day will declare it, because it will be revealed by fire, and the fire will test what sort of work each has done" (1 Corinthians 3:13). In Revelation 3:18, Jesus counseled the church of Laodicea to buy from Him gold refined in the fire so they would be rich. We can only be as pure gold when we have been tested by fire.

Back to the kitchen, do you want to be a maker of cereal, or do you want to cook for hundreds? God has enough cereal makers, what He needs is a few refined chefs.

God in Heaven. Welcome me into Your kitchen and show me what You would have me do. I pray I would be delivered from Your refining fire as pure gold. Amen.

> *I have spoken these things to you, that My joy may remain in you, and that your joy may be full.* (John 15:11)

LYRA'S JOY

I've heard it said that being a grandparent is different than being a parent. Now that I am "Poppa," – the name my twin grandkids gave me – I will admit that there is a difference between the two. Not that it's better or worse, just different. Just as we are the legacy of our parents and our grandparents, our children and their children are our legacy. Our DNA, the fingerprint of our lives, lives on through them. When we leave this world, a small part of us continues through our offspring.

Whenever I stop by my daughter and son-in-law's house for a visit, I often arrive empty-handed but, from time-to-time, I will have a little something for the grands. As I said earlier, they *are* twins but they are two different people. You see, one is a boy, Josh, and Lyra, well she is a little girl. As you might suspect, not only are they different genders, each has their own unique personality. While they are both happy with whatever I bring, they are different kinds of happy.

Josh will take the gift from me, look at it a few seconds, say, "Thank you, Poppa," then go back to whatever he was doing. Lyra, on the other hand, will come up to me, look at the bag in my hand, and ask, "Whatcha' got in the bag, Poppa? You got new shoes for Sissy?"

"I don't know, you had better look and see," is my usual reply.

She will take the bag from me and pull out whatever I brought. She will take the item, show it to Heather (their mother, my forever Punkin), and tell her, "Look what Poppa brought Sissy, Momma." Then, without fail, she will pull whatever the item is up to her face and she will smell it. Not just a little sniff, but she will inhale as deeply as she can through her little nose. I asked her why she smells everything and she told me, "Cause you gived it to me, Poppa." I'm guessing that's her way of enjoying every bit of the gift-receiving experience.

As a Christian, I am reminded that Lyra's full-body experience is an example of how we should receive every gift that God gives us. If I receive some pleasure by observing Lyra's joy and exuberance because of some little thing I've given her, why would I not want to let God know that I am equally as thankful for all His daily gifts? Yet, I must confess that I sometimes take these gifts (simple to some, a miracle in reality) for granted.

We must remember that every day we awaken, every bite of food we eat, every drop of water we drink, and every breath of air we breathe, are gifts from God. Next time, instead of a quick, "Thank You, God," I need to reach out to Him, take the gift, lift it to my face, and breathe it in to the fullest. I must remember that whatever gift it is deserves as much recognition as I can muster. Why? Because He gived it to me.

Father God. While I may not show it all the time, I am truly thankful for every one of Your gifts. Amen.

> *But, according to His promise, we are waiting for new heavens and a new earth, in which righteousness dwells.* (2 Peter 3:13)

OUR PROMISED FUTURE

We like to make plans. If you walk down the aisles of office supply stores, you will eventually come to a section filled with planners. You'll find day planners, weekly planners, monthly planners, and yearly planners. When we work, we are planning years into the future for a retirement we all hope to enjoy. Some people make their living as wedding planners, event planners, activity planners, and all sorts of other things that promise to be the next "big thing."

Years ago, our family drove to Washington D.C. to see our nation's capital. History came alive to the eleven-year-old boy that was me. I saw buildings that, until that trip, had only existed as pictures from books and magazines. We saw the Capitol Building, the Washington and Lincoln monuments, and a small part of the Smithsonian Museum. On our return trip, we drove through North Carolina's outer banks. We saw Kitty Hawk, the sight of man's first powered flight (all 120 feet of it). Our plan was to catch the ferry that connects Hatteras Island to Ocracoke Island. As I've learned many times since that trip, plans for the future don't always work out.

Our trip was going without a hitch. Having never been on a ferry, I was looking forward to crossing that stretch of water on a boat that was big enough to carry cars. I had never seen a boat that big, and I wanted to see it. The one thing my parents didn't take into account when they planned this trip was the ferry schedule. Oh, I did get to see that big boat. I saw it as it powered its way southward toward the horizon. You see, we got there just a little late. Much to my disappointment, we loaded back into the family sedan and drove back the way we had come, found a hotel on the North Carolina mainland, and resumed our trip home the following day. So much for plans.

As Christians, we constantly remind ourselves – and others – that we are not promised our next heartbeat or breath. Because we are saved, we know that either Jesus is returning to us or we are going to Him. And it is with that promised future that we Christians should be happy to spread the good news so others can join the family. According to Peter, God wants all to join Him in heaven. "But He is patient with us, because He does not want any to perish, but all to come to repentance" (2 Peter 3:9b). If that is the wish of God, we should desire the same. "Witness to One, Share with All," should be the motto of every Christian.

As we watched that ferry steam southward, having a backup plan would have been a good thing. But when it comes to eternity, there's no such thing as a backup plan. One of two futures is waiting for all of us. I have planned for mine; I must help others plan for theirs. That's one boat we don't want to miss.

Lord God. Thank You for revealing Your eternal plan for us, Your greatest creation. Even though we don't deserve it, Your plan includes sharing Your eternal home with those who believe and repent of their sins and receive Your gift of eternal salvation. I pray that You would open the mouths of the saved and the ears of the unbelieving so all will come to know You. Amen.

> *Do not judge according to appearance, but practice righteous judgment.* (John 7:24)

NOT WHAT I EXPECTED

Asparagus. For many years, I resisted eating this vegetable. Actually, I wouldn't even taste it. Why not? Because I had convinced myself that I knew what it would taste like. I knew I didn't like what I thought it tasted like even though I had never actually had so much as a single taste. Oh, I hear you. I hear you telling me, "That's a closed-minded way to go through life." I know you are thinking that because that's exactly what I would be thinking if I were the one reading this account.

Why do we – at least I – have this mindset? Because at one time in our lives, we had formed an opinion about something and when we actually encountered that something, our initial opinion proved to be accurate. That opinion may or may not have been influenced by input from others but it was our opinion and we were convinced that it was correct. Using that logic, any future opinion we formed was correct until proven otherwise.

As I've grown older – and a bit wiser – I've learned that while some books may match their cover, most do not. A few years ago, I was eating lunch at a local restaurant with a group of friends. One of my workmates ordered asparagus and he convinced me to give it a try. I gave in and, much to my surprise, I discovered that asparagus wasn't half bad. As a matter of fact, it is now one of my go-to vegetables. Salmon hasn't always been one of those "I want to eat" foods, but, in my opinion, you would be hard pressed to find a grilled fish that is any better.

We Christians are, to a lot of the world, a book that is to be judged. The unsaved may look at us and form an opinion based on an observation of other Christians or, most likely, their opinion is based on input from the devil. We can tell them that following Christ is when we truly began to live life. We try to explain that it is only when you surrender total control that you find ultimate victory.

While asparagus always tasted like asparagus, I had to personally experience it to find out I like asparagus. Someone who has never sampled sugar will never be able to comprehend sweet until they actually allow some sugar to contact their tongue. The only way to ensure ultimate victory over death is to surrender our lives to Christ, right now, while we are still alive.

Yes, it's true that if I had never tasted asparagus, I would have never known that I like asparagus. But in the end, my liking asparagus really doesn't matter. If you aren't a Christian, it may not matter to you right now, but in the end, you're going to spend your entire eternity wishing you had just given it a try. Don't be like me; don't spend an entire lifetime not knowing what you are missing. You should give the asparagus a try, and give your life to Christ.

Eternal Savior. Thank You for the gift that is asparagus and all of the other food You created for us to enjoy. I pray that the unsaved will take the time to learn how they can become one of Your children so they can enjoy all of the good that is waiting for them in their heavenly home. Amen.

> *Proclaim His glory among the nations, His wonders among all peoples.* (Psalm 96:3)

SPOILER ALERT

"That's a good book." I was having my vehicle serviced and was waiting at the dealership. As I walked through the spacious waiting area, I saw an older man sitting in one of the overstuffed chairs. On the arm of his chair was a book I had recently finished. Although it took a chapter of two to really get started, once I got into it, I literally couldn't put it down until I read the last page. It was one of those books that didn't give away the "who done it" until the final couple of pages. Had I been a spoiler, I might have added, "You're gonna like the ending. I would never have believed she killed him."

Spoilers. We all know someone who simply can't – or won't – keep a secret. I was in a theater watching a movie and the couple behind me had already seen the film. There were enough plot twists to constantly keep me guessing as to what was about to happen. Or it would have. The couple behind me kept saying, loud enough for several people to hear, what the next turn in the road would reveal. Tired of hearing them, I changed seats so I would be out of earshot of the spoilers. My new seat wasn't as good, but at least I had something to look forward to for the remainder of the film.

No one likes a spoiler. We want to discover, on our own, what happens in the book we are reading or the movie we paid good money to see. Someone telling you what lies ahead can take away the enjoyment you feel when you make your own discovery. But in life, a spoiler for certain things would often save us time, money, and heartache. How many times have I said, "If I could just go back to my twenties knowing what I know now, I would be a lot better off"?

I remember playing golf with some friends at a course familiar to them but not to me. I had the honors so I had the tee box. Seeing the flag in the distance, I decided that I would attempt to drive the green, or at least get close. After hitting a particularly good tee shot, I turned to my playing partners and asked if they saw that shot. They said they had seen it, but they told me that I'd need a ball when I got down there. "Why? It's right in the middle of the fairway." What they knew that I didn't was that the hill between the tee box and the green hid a small pond. Why didn't they tell me? They didn't want to spoil my fun. Ha ha.

As Christians, if we believe what the Bible says, we know how the story ends. We know Satan only stops his scheming when he is cast into the eternal abyss that is hell. We know heaven awaits those who have accepted God's gift of eternal salvation. We know what we have to do to be saved and spared an eternity of separation from God. We know about heaven being a place where, "Night shall be no more. They need no lamp nor the light of the sun, for the Lord God will give them light" (Revelation 22:5a). We also know that Jesus, in Mark 16:15, tells us to tell the whole world about the good news of the Gospel.

No, the man I saw at the car dealership wasn't reading the Bible. And no, I didn't tell him how the book ended. I didn't want to spoil his reading. But when it comes to telling others about eternal salvation, Jesus expects us to spoil it for Satan and to tell everyone we see.

Lord Jesus. Thank You for the gift of salvation we can have because of what You did on Calvary. Let us obey Your command and tell the world so Satan's schemes can be spoiled. Amen.

> *Beloved, do not imitate that which is evil, but that which is good. Whoever does good is from God, but whoever does evil has not seen God.* (3 John 11)

THE FLATTERY OF IMITATION

Any man, including myself, who was interested in anything when he was a boy, had people whose behavior he wanted to model. If it was baseball, that young boy probably had a few players he would imitate, even down to the way his hero walked to the plate or wore his cap. As a one-time golfer, I can give you a list of players who would be worthy models to follow: Jack Nicklaus, Tiger Woods, Phil Michelson, Gary Player, Ernie Els, or Fred Couples, just to name a few. All these, and many more, are great golfers, and between them all, they have won hundreds of professional golf tournaments. If someone could successfully copy any of those golf swings and had a modest amount of ability, that person would be very happy on a golf course.

But how about their lives away from golf? While Tiger Woods is one of the best to have ever played the game, some say the best ever, he hasn't enjoyed quite the same success in his personal life. None of us would want our lives displayed to the same degree as today's celebrities, and I would imagine those celebrities wished they could simply have a normal life outside of their chosen profession. But, because their private lives are open to us, we know that we wouldn't want to make the same personal decisions that Tiger has made.

As a Christian, we are also under a microscope. The world is constantly looking at us, wanting to hear us use the language that is acceptable by the world but not by our God. Wherever you find yourself, you can bet that someone is watching and listening for our next bad decision or action. Would Jesus look in our direction, point to us, and tell someone, "That's the example you should follow if you want to live the life I tell you to live"?

As followers of Christ, we must remember these words from the New Testament: "There is no creature that is not revealed in His sight, for all things are bare and exposed to the eyes of Him to whom we must give account" (Hebrews 4:13). The world may see our actions, but God knows our motives. The world hears our words, but God knows our thoughts. When we read these words of John, "Whoever says he remains in Him ought to walk as He walked" (1 John 2:6), we learn that we must imitate the life of Jesus.

If you want to hit a baseball, imitate a professional. If you want to do well on a golf course, imitate a professional. As a fisherman, I want to catch fish like Bobby Lane, Kevin Vandam, Andy Montgomery, Edwin Evers, Jordan Lee, or Bill Dance. But, as a Christian, I want to live like Jesus. He's the only example I need.

Lord Jesus. I pray that I will always ask myself what You would do in any situation in which I find myself. I pray I will remember that I may be the only part of You that someone sees and that I would show enough of You for them to want more of You in their lives. Amen.

> *Therefore, brothers, let it be known to you that through this Man forgiveness of sins is proclaimed to you.* (Acts 13:38)

I FORGIVE... ME

Grudges. Grudges are a truly terrible thing. When you say you are holding a grudge, you are lying to both the world and to yourself. You don't hold the grudge; it holds you. A grudge will eat at you from the inside. To the outside world, you may appear fine, but that grudge is doing its best to destroy you. Most people know this, so we do our best to forgive others. To sum up Colossians 3:13, we must forgive others because God forgave us. So we forgive them. As for me, I find that forgiving others frees me of resentment, bitterness, anger, and other unhealthy things that can eat away my happiness. As a matter of fact, I can forgive pretty much anyone for pretty much anything, except . . .

When we forgive someone, we are to forgive exactly as God has forgiven us. Because we are human and we are not God, we can do the forgiveness thing pretty well, but it's the forgetting thing we have trouble with. But, if we are to live our life as a Christian, we must not let that transgression affect any future relationship we have with the person we say we have forgiven. We can't, no, not strong enough; we *must* never bring it up again. It must be as though it never happened. And I can do that for pretty much anyone, except . . .

As I've grown older – I'm now over sixty – I've come to realize that the hardest person in my life to forgive is no stranger and doesn't live life waiting to "get me back." The hardest person in my life to forgive lives in my mirror. When I look in my mirror, I struggle to see someone who is worthy, in the least imaginable of ways, of being forgiven of the terrible things I have done, said, or thought. I look at my reflection and ask the same question I've asked so many times before, "Why would God forgive you?"

Sensing an opportunity, my ancient foe, Lucifer, whispers in my ear, "You're right, you aren't worthy of forgiveness. When I think of all the times you've done what I wanted, I must say you being a smile to my face. Why should God forgive you when you can't even forgive yourself?"

After I've heard all I want to hear, I tell Lucifer to hush. I remind him that the same God created both him AND me. Then I ask him a question. I ask him if he knows the two differences between him and me. "One difference between you and me is that I know I'm not worthy of His forgiveness. The other difference between you and me is that I know I'm forgiven."

There's not a day that goes by that Satan doesn't tell me I'm not worthy of Jesus' forgiveness. He may be the master of lies but one thing he says is true: I'm not worthy, at least according to me. You see, that's one of the differences between Jesus and me. In my heart, I'm not worthy of being forgiven. I'm glad Jesus doesn't listen to me because in His heart, I am.

Lord Jesus. Thank You for Your forgiveness of my sins. I ask You to help me forgive myself. Amen.

> *And whatever you do in word or deed, do all in the name of the Lord Jesus, giving thanks to God the Father through Him.*
> (Colossians 3:17)

BEING ALL IN

I'm in. Two small words that mean so much. When I say, "I'm in," I am telling someone that I will be there. Someone who says they are in means they can be counted on to do whatever it is that needs being done. Their word has been given and the expectation is they will honor their word. One caveat to being in, we usually want to know what it is that we are being asked to do. In other words, our being in often comes with conditions.

Pretend you are a golfer and you get a call asking if you are available Friday morning for a round with the guys. You've penciled something in, but it can be rearranged if the right opportunity comes up. "Where?" you ask. When you hear the magical words, "Shoal Creek," you immediately discount whatever that menial task was. Before the "k" in Creek is sounded, you affirm that you are in. Now, let's say the same friend is calling, but this time, instead of asking about a round of golf, he asks if you can help three friends move a few things. Suddenly, that menial task takes on a whole new level of importance. "I'd love to help, but I can't," you answer, "I have a project that has to be finished."

If you're ever flipping through the guide on your television, there's a chance you will find a televised poker game. If you've ever watched one of these shows, eventually you will hear the phrase, "I'm *all in*," as the player pushes their entire pile of chips to the center of the table. In poker, being *all in* is to win it all or to lose it all. Regardless of the outcome, you have made your declaration.

To be a Christian is to be *all in*. "If anyone serves Me, he must follow Me. Where I am, there will My servant be also. If anyone serves Me, the Father will honor him" (John 12:26). Jesus is telling us that we must be *all in* if we want to serve Him. If you doubt His demand that we be *all in*, read these words from Matthew, "And he who does not take his cross and follow after Me is not worthy of Me" (Matthew

10:38). I don't know about you but to me, Jesus sounds like He expects us to be *all in*.

The problem with being partially in is that we are partially out. Jesus goes on to say, "He who finds his life will lose it, and he who loses his life for My sake will find it" (Matthew 10:39). Jesus wants us to be a 100%, *all in*, Christian. He doesn't want someone to be content with just being a *nearly in* or a *partially in* Christian. He doesn't want us to watch from the sideline, He wants us to get in the game. If the world should ask why we do the things we do or say the things we say, our answer should always be that we are an *all in* Christian.

The cards for your eternity have been dealt and you are seated at the table. The question you must answer is, "Are you in or are you out?" Jesus went *all in* for us. If you hear that question from Him, without hesitation, put your cards down, push your chips to the middle of the table, and announce with a loud voice for all to hear, "I'm *all in*."

Eternal Savior. Thank You for going all in for me. I pray that I would be willing go all in for You. Amen.

For My thoughts are not your thoughts, nor are your ways My ways, says the Lord. For as the heavens are higher than the earth, so are My ways higher than your ways, and My thoughts than your thoughts. (Isaiah 55:8-9)

HERE, LET ME EXPLAIN

At my job, I am fortunate to work with some of the smartest people I know. While none of them know everything there is to know about what we do, I know I can ask a question, and someone will give me a knowledgeable answer. I also know some people who need the following caveat: "I don't need to know everything, just summarize it." When it comes to explaining how something works, most of the time, all I need to know is what can be found in the kiddie pool of knowledge. While I'm content with wading in the knee-deep water, there are some who are pulling me to the high dive, ready to jump into the deep end.

Some humans are born curious. You know the type. They see something and they immediately want to take it apart to see what makes it tick. I'll admit that there are times I see something and I think, "I wonder what makes that thing do what it does?" As I've grown older, I've learned there are many things I don't understand and probably never will. There are questions I will never be able to answer. And even if I could know everything, I'm pretty sure I wouldn't want to. I don't have to understand aerodynamics; I just need to know the plane's gonna fly.

When it comes to my eternal salvation, I will never fully understand why God chose to save me, but I'm eternally grateful that He did. Sure, there are things I would like to ask God, but most of those are things I know I'm not meant to know. Age has taught me the wisdom of a few words from the child's song, *Jesus Loves Me*: "Jesus loves me, this I know, for the Bible tells me so."

Based on experience, I can tell you how to build an effective presentation. I can explain keyboard shortcuts, how to ground a transmission line, and how to fly a four-stringed stunt kite. I can tell you what I know about fishing, and I can tell you how to bake some pretty good cookies or a cobbler. When it comes to salvation, I can tell you what the Bible says in First John about how you can be saved: "If we confess our sins, He is faithful and just to forgive us our sins and cleanse us from all unrighteousness" (1 John 1:9). But if you ask me why, why would God do that even after I have disappointed Him countless times? My answer, as simplistic as this may sound, is: "Because He loves me."

Like I said, I can't explain everything, but when it comes to why God would save me, for me, John 3:16 is explanation enough. Because He loves me.

Dear Jesus. If I could, I could never say, "I'm sorry" enough to justify Your death on that cross. I will never understand why You looked at me and said, "Him too." I know You didn't need to save me for Your benefit; You saved me for my benefit, and You saved me because I couldn't. Amen.

> *He blotted out the handwriting of ordinances that was against us and contrary to us, and He took it out of the way, nailing it to the cross.* (Colossians 2:14)

CANCELLED

Who among us has not spent at least a few moments looking ahead to a certain wonderful day sometime in our future? While no one fully knows what their future holds, according to James 4:14, we cannot know with 100% certainty what will happen within the next 24 hours, so why do we spend so much time daydreaming about years into the future? Well, if all goes as it is going, about eight years from now, I will write one final check that will pay off my home mortgage. If you don't have a mortgage, chances are you have a car note (or truck, or boat, or motorcycle, etc.), some student loans, a medical debt, or some other large debt you are working toward paying off.

Debt can be overwhelming. It can suffocate your life. Debt has destroyed relationships and permanently scarred reputations. But, like many of the troubles in our lives, debt typically doesn't happen all by itself. Debt usually needs our permission, cooperation, and consent before it can grow to humongous proportions. Debt can easily become one of those devils in our life, causing us to divert time and other resources to it rather than to the things of God.

Just as we have financial obligations that must be paid, each of us has a sin debt that also must be accounted for. The difference in cash debt and sin debt is that sin is held not over our head but over our soul. At the end of our life, each of us will be accountable for a sin debt certificate that is stamped with the words, "Paid in Full on [enter date here]." We can try to deny owing it, try to run from it, pretend it doesn't exist, or ignore it, hoping it will somehow be forgotten, lost in the pile of all of the other sin debt of the world.

But sin can't be reasoned with; by itself, sin never goes away. Once we have made a withdrawal from the bank of sin, we are in debt to that bank forever. Sin is the one debt that *we* can never repay, and Satan knows that. Once we have "borrowed" from his eternal and never satisfied bank of sin, we are in his debt forever and he will do whatever he can to make sure we pay that debt with our eternal soul. He knows that each time we try to rid ourselves of that sin, we are just spinning our wheels, but he tells us, "Don't give up, you were thissss close." You see, Satan holds all of the sin, but he holds none of the forgiveness.

When we realize there is no way we, on our own, can erase that debt, we must then go to the only one who can. Jesus established the eternal path to debt forgiveness on a hill outside of Jerusalem when He put your forgiveness note in His bank through His death, burial, and resurrection. We don't have to plead our case and we don't have to justify the reason for our sin; we just have to ask that the debt be cancelled.

Yes, one day I will send in my last and final house payment. It will have taken 18 years to write that final check. As for my sin debt, it only took one payment, it cost me nothing, and through that payment, I gained everything.

My Savior and Lord Jesus. Thank You for the forgiveness of my sin debt. I know You paid a debt I could not pay. From an unworthy but ever grateful heart, thank You. Amen.

Again, Jesus spoke to them, saying, "I am the light of the world. Whoever follows Me shall not walk in the darkness, but shall have the light of life." (John 8:12)

FOLLOWING YOUR SHADOW

Have you ever thought about shadows? Shadows can be unsettling or they can be comforting. Shadows can tell the time or they can warn of danger lurking around the corner. I once saw a video of Raymond Crowe, an Australian magician, as he performed a shadow puppet routine to Louis Armstrong's famous tune, *What a Wonderful World*. While that may not sound so special, if you have a couple of minutes, I'm sure you can find it on the Internet. I may be easily impressed, but in my opinion, Mr. Crowe is an impressive manipulator of light and shadow. We can be accused of chasing shadows, boxers often tweak their skills by shadow boxing, or one can dance with their shadow. Shadows are one part of life often overlooked.

When I see my shadow, I know a few things. One, I know that I'm alive and am able to greet another day. Two, there's a light source somewhere that allows me to have a shadow. I have found that the farther my light source is behind me, the longer my shadow is in front of me. Suppose I am looking at the shadow of my Christian life. If my shadow extends far ahead of me, what does that say about me and how I'm living my life?

As a Christian, John 8:12 plainly tells me that Jesus is my light. If I read further in the New Testament, I find this passage, "But if we walk in the light as He is in the light, we have fellowship one with another" (1 John 1:7a). If I take a second to think about the physics of how a shadow works and I can see my Christian shadow leading the way, it shouldn't take but a second to realize I'm doing it wrong. I must remember the words of Jesus from my opening verse when He said, "Whoever *follows* Me."

If I can see my shadow, my light source is behind me. If Jesus is behind me, then I cannot follow Him. If I insist on leading the way, I may find myself stepping in Satan's potholes of temptation because my shadow is blocking my view. If I keep tripping over Satan's temptations, eventually I'm going to have to step aside and let Jesus lead my way. Yes, it's good to have Jesus at my side to help me to my feet when I stumble and fall, but life is so much easier if I let Him lead my steps and light my path.

The next time I see my shadow creeping toward the front of my walk, I need to realize that I have, once again, started to take the lead. I'm sorry, Jesus, why don't You lead the way.

Lord Jesus. Let me remember that You are the light, not only of the world, but of my life. I pray that the next time I am tempted to take the lead, You will tap me on the shoulder and tell me to slow down so You can, once again, light my path. Amen.

Then He said to them all, "If anyone will come after Me, let him deny himself, and take up his cross daily, and follow Me.
(Luke 9:23)

ONE DAY AT A TIME

Every day, each of us has a job that we must do. It seems that every time we think we can finally see the light at the end of the tunnel, something unforeseen surfaces that we are forced to address. Whether it be car trouble, sick children, being asked to help aging parents, or new responsibilities at work, it seems there is no shortage of new "opportunities" needing our immediate attention. Still, I will admit that there are days that I hardly do anything.

House cleaning and laundry can wait, I'll bathe the dogs next week, I'll pay those bills tomorrow. Whatever the chore, sometimes it has to wait. From time-to-time, we all need to kick back and recharge our batteries. What's the problem with recharging our batteries? While we were recharging, those things that needed doing never got around to doing themselves. What I didn't do today will need to be done tomorrow. And when tomorrow gets here, I must add the things I didn't do yesterday to the things waiting to be done.

Being a Christian is one of those everyday things we must do every single day. Each day, we are called to take up our cross, whatever that cross may be, and live each day as Jesus would have us live. Each day, we must deny that thing that we may want to do and ask Jesus what it is He wants us to do. The thing about asking Jesus what He wants us to do is that we must be willing to do something.

You've been waiting for three months for this version of the "game of the century" and now the day of the game is finally here. You ask God what He wants and, sure enough, He wants you to do something for one of your neighbors. It's not the "what" that bothers you; it's the "when."

"But God," you plead, doing your best Moses interpretation when God spoke to him through a fiery bush, "that's when the game will start." The game will be played regardless of your attendance or attention. If God wants you to do something while the game is played, that is the cross you must bear.

Following God is not always easy. Following God's plan may not always correspond to your calendar or schedule. Following God probably will not end up with you receiving fortune or fame. It's probable that whatever you do for God's kingdom will never be noticed by those around you. But you can rest assured that what you do in God's name or for His kingdom will be noticed by Him. We will most likely not see the fruit that comes from the heavenly seeds we plant. Being a Christian doesn't come with an off day; being a Christian is a seven-day-a-week, twenty-four-hours-a-day thing.

For every one of our days, there is a cross we must bear. What we are called to do is to stop, bend down, and pick it up. It won't be too heavy; Jesus understands all about carrying crosses. He's been there, and He's done that.

Eternal Father and Lord. I pray that You will make me willing to bear the cross You would have me carry. Amen.

The words of his mouth were smoother than butter, but battle was in his heart; his words were softer than oil, yet they were drawn swords. (Psalm 55:21)

STICKS AND STONES

"Sticks and stones may break my bones, but words will never hurt me." Who, among us, has never made or heard that childhood declaration? If you're thinking this phrase was originally said to deflect criticism, bullying, or other playground taunts, you would be correct. Although there is no definitive source of the phrase, it has found its way into our daily language. While we know the intent of the phrase, ask yourself, "Is it really true?"

One of the things I tell people when I ask for an opinion about something is that they can't hurt my feelings. I assure people that, "I have one feeling that can be hurt and it's locked up in a box at home." I tell them this because I want honest feedback. But can words hurt? I'll answer that query with single word: "Yes."

When we think of a betrayal, we may think of an action (remember the Judas kiss?), but that action usually began with some words. Ask a person who has been falsely accused of something if words hurt. If you have ever heard the phrase, "But we can still be friends," I'm sure you will contest the final six words – "but words will never hurt me" – of that childhood phrase. Marriages have ended, business partnerships torn apart, reputations ruined, relationships disbanded, and family feuds started, all because of a few, hurtful words.

The Bible tells us that the thoughts of our hearts leave us as words from our mouth. Words cut deeper than to the bone; words cut to the heart. When we are wounded by the words of others, Satan tells us to strike while the iron is hot. "Are you going to let her get away with that?" he may ask, or we also might hear this from his devilish lips: "I wouldn't take that if I were you." We find in Matthew that, "But I say to you that for every idle word that men speak, they will give an account on the Day of Judgment" (Matthew 12:36). I don't know about you, but that gets my attention.

While words can kill dreams, words can also heal. Ephesians 4:29 tells us our words should build up so we may give grace to those who hear. Think of the worst thing that someone has ever said to you. You may have been accused of something you didn't do or you may have received a tongue-lashing that was meant for someone else; you just happened to be a convenient target when the words were released. When we reason that we are justified to lash back, we must remember something that was said from the top of a hill nearly 2,000 years ago, "Father, forgive them."

Yes, sticks and stones hurt, and they can injure; they can even kill. The words we speak can either hurt the heart, or, if we want, heal old wounds. "Let the words of my mouth and the meditation of my heart be acceptable in Your sight, O Lord, my strength and my redeemer" (Psalm 19:14).

Lord God. I pray that You would guard my heart against thoughts that could leave me as hurtful words. Give me the strength to forgive before forgiveness is needed because of a few harmful words. Amen.

And since they did not see fit to acknowledge God, God gave them over to a debased mind, to do those things which are not proper. (Romans 1:28)

YOUR THOUGHT CUP

If you are like me, you take time each morning to read from God's Word. I have discovered that reading the Bible at the beginning of each day gets me off to a good start. In addition to reading the Bible, I also begin each day enjoying another of God's gifts, coffee. I'm not a big coffee drinker but I normally have two cups, one as I read and the other as I drive to work.

My work cup (the second of the day) is one of the now-popular stainless-steel tumblers that ensures that the coffee remains hot until I finish the full 20 ounces. Each day, I normally sip my first cup from the same ceramic mug (I wash it each night), but there are times I will use any of a number of other mugs. All of these are ceramic but, because of their uniquely individual shapes, each of them holds a slightly different amount. Regardless of the capacity, I have found that each mug will only hold as much as it will hold.

Some people will tell me that God intended us to drink our coffee black with no additives. Been there, tried that. I have to have a bit of cream and some sweetener to enjoy my coffee. Let's suppose I fill my mug to the brim with coffee. Let us further suppose that I then add some of the sweet stuff and then the cream. What do you think will have happened? If you said that I made a mess, you would be correct. I made the mess because the combination of the coffee PLUS the sweetener PLUS the cream was more than my cup was intended to hold, and my once-clean countertop now had coffee on it. Now I have a mess to clean, because why? Because I attempted to add something to a cup that was already filled with something else.

We all have a "thought cup" that, each day, begins as an empty vessel. Almost from the moment we first awaken, that cup begins to fill with thoughts. We think about what we will do today or what we didn't get done yesterday. Money issues find their way into the cup as do relationship things, school, work, health, or a number of other pressing issues. If we continue to fill our cup with the things of this world, before long we will find there is no room for the things of God. Suppose our cup is filled with thoughts of God. Before we know it, the world begins to creep its way into the cup, forcing us to replace our God thoughts with world thoughts. When our God thoughts and our thoughts of the world begin to spill from the cup, is it any wonder we often make such a mess of our lives?

Life will force us to think about it throughout the day. Satan will tempt us with frustrations, temptations, greed, pride, and anger. As we wind our way throughout each day, let us make sure that we take time to dip the world from our cup so that our cup will always have room for the thoughts of God. After all, He always has room for us.

Father in heaven. Thank You for all of Your gifts, including Your Word and coffee. Let me not have a cup that is so filled with the stuff of this world that I don't have room for You in my thoughts and life. Amen.

Jesus answered him, "Truly, truly I say to you, unless a man is born again, he cannot see the kingdom of God." (John 3:3)

KEEP IT SIMPLE

You're working a crossword puzzle and you need an eleven-letter word for "opposite of simple." Complicated. Problematic. Let's make that simpler; you need a four-letter word that is the antonym of simple. Antonym? That's a hard word to define. Hard! That's it. While there are things in life that are not easy, we humans tend to make most things harder than they have to be. For instance, some people say antonym instead of opposite. As of this writing, with life seemingly in a constant state of uncertainty caused by the COVID-19 virus, think of any word that is the antonym of simple and you can pretty much define our present set of circumstances. Even without this new invisible enemy, life, because of another, much older, invisible enemy can be hard.

Life, it has been said, is not for sissies. There are bills to pay, jobs to work (so we can pay those bills), kids needing attention, places to go, people to see, and things to do. Have you ever wondered if life is hard because we make it so or is it simply hard?

Several times during my Sunday school teaching years, we would sit the group of children in a line of chairs and whisper a short sentence to a child on one end of the line. That child would turn to their side, whisper what they thought they heard to the next child and the process would repeat itself until the last child would repeat what they heard. Often, the sentence the final child repeated would be nothing like the sentence that began the game.

For a moment, let's look at the Bible. From Genesis 1:1 to Revelation 22:21, there are thousands of words that make up God's Holy Word. Because of the different languages used when the words were first written, some of the passages can be a challenge to understand. But when you read the entire Bible, at its simplest, the Bible tells us this: God is God and He created everything; Jesus is God's Son; God and Jesus love us; and God wants us to be with Him in heaven when we leave this earth. On the other hand, Satan hates us and we sin when we follow Satan instead of God. We can't get to heaven because of our sin. God had a plan for that, but Jesus had to die for our sins so we could have a way into heaven. We deserve eternal death, but we can have eternal life if we ask God to forgive us of those sins.

Yes, life can be hard but getting into heaven is, when you think about it, fairly simple. Admit your sins, believe Jesus died and rose from the tomb, ask for forgiveness, and confess that Jesus Christ is Lord above all. There are a lot of words in the Bible, but it simply says this: God loves us. That's simple enough for me.

Father God and Jesus. I thank You for the simple message of Your love for us that is in the Bible. I pray that we would keep Your message simple when we tell others so they could also understand that heaven has a room especially for them. Amen.

Being submissive to one another in the fear of God.
(Ephesians 5:21)

DARING TO SUBMIT

Let's face it; we sometimes like to pick and choose those Bible verses that best suit our immediate needs. I know some husbands who have claimed three verses from Ephesians chapter five as their personal, catch all, verses. Verses 22, 23, and 24 plainly state that a wife is to submit to her husband because he is the head of the house just as Jesus is head of the church. Since the church is to yield to the head – Jesus, in that husband's mind, the wife is to yield to him, no questions asked. For some men, those three verses pretty much sum up what the marital relationship should be; they say jump and she asks how high and where would his majesty like for her to land?

Wouldn't that be grand, to have someone submit to your every command without questioning your motive simply because you said so? Your judgment is final and should not be questioned because it's right there in the Bible, you are the head. Hmm. Sounds like a slight misunderstanding and a cherry picking of what we want.

If we're honest, none of us truly like to submit. All of us were born with a rebellious spirit. To submit is – to the rebellious mind – to relinquish our freedom and our control of the things we say and do. As long as we hold on to our rebellious spirit, none of us, be we a husband, a wife, a parent, a child, whatever; very few people, if any, want to totally give up their freedom to do as they choose. We don't want to yield to anyone. But, in each of our lives, there comes a time when we must answer the question: Are we going to rebel or are we going to follow?

To be a Christian means we must submit to the will of Christ and God. We may like looking through the Bible to find verses that best suit our need, but to be a Christian means we must submit to the entire Bible, not just the "good" verses. Those three verses from Ephesians may sound good, but look forward just a bit. "Husbands, love your wives, just as Christ also loved the church" and "In this way men ought to love their wives as their own bodies" (Ephesians 5:25a, 28a).

When we submit, we find ourselves being obedient to God and Jesus. Only by submitting will we be able to show the world that we are under the control of God's Holy Spirit who now lives within us. Jesus could have avoided the cross – if He had submitted to His will instead of the will of His Father. Submission sometimes requires us to miss out on some things but, in the end, we will receive more reward than our earthly minds can imagine.

Submission is not always what we want to do, but it is always what we must do. And don't worry, if submission is the key to fulfillment, God will give you the strength to submit.

Eternal God. I pray that You will forgive me for those times when I don't submit to You and Your will. I pray that You will give me the wisdom, courage, and strength so I will be able to know Your will and to resist my natural spirit of rebellion.
Amen.

The Lord has made all things for Himself...
(Proverbs 16:4a)

CREATED TO BE

Think about some of the things you have sitting around your house. Kitchen cabinets and drawers contain bowls, plates, utensils, and paper towels. Look in other areas of that kitchen and you will most likely find food in a refrigerator or pantry. Somewhere in your house is at least one computer. Closets and dresser drawers contain clothes, towels, shoes, socks, and sleep clothes. Every night and morning, you visit the bathroom, retrieve a toothbrush, apply a little dab of toothpaste, and brush your teeth. From the simplest to the most complex, each of these, and every other item you use, was created to perform a defined task.

A lot of those items, because of a specific need, are called upon to do something other than its intended purpose. Take a fork. The typical fork is intended to serve a single purpose: to transport food from my plate to my mouth. I don't know about you but I use forks for other things. Forks are excellent for scrambling eggs and for crimping the edge of dough when I make fried apple pies.

We often re-purpose things after they have served their original purpose. I have a complete set of juice glasses that began their life as candle containers. I'm not sure if the designer of the little glass envisioned me sipping pineapple orange juice from their creation, but those retired candle holders sure do a fine job of playing the part of a juice glass.

We are like that little glass. Each of us was born with an intended purpose. Some knew from an early age what their vocation would be when they grew up, but most of us had no idea. I know a few people well into their fifties or even sixties who are still trying to figure out just exactly what it is they were born to do. Unfortunately, if someone is looking to the world to show them what they were put on this earth to do, they are barking up the wrong tree.

All of us were born to worship God, but God gave each of us unique talents that He wants us to use in His service. Some can cook, others can teach, sing, or write. If I were to use that small glass as a shooting target instead of a juice glass, it would work, but only once. I would have ruined a perfectly good glass because I didn't realize the true potential of that small glass container.

When we ask God to reveal our purpose in this life, He will show us. It may not be what we want, but we will find that when we follow God's will, that's when we will most likely fulfill that destiny we are seeking. But if we ignore God's will, we may one day find ourselves broken and scattered about in pieces like that target of a juice glass, shot down by the world and its demands.

Knowing your purpose is not always easy. Instead of worrying about knowing our purpose, let's work on knowing God. He'll tell us our purpose when He's ready.

Father God. I pray that I will listen to You when You tell me what it is You want me to do. I thank You for the gifts I have received, and I pray that You are satisfied with my efforts for Your service. Amen.

> *A prudent man foresees the evil and hides himself, but the simple pass on and are punished.* (Proverbs 27:12)

KNOWING THE COST

"Don't make me take my belt off!" Whoo! Even at sixty years old, when I remember those seven words, I wonder what it was that made Daddy think I wanted him to him take his belt off. Why would I actually want to make him do something that was going to cause me pain and suffering? Now, before your thinking goes down the wrong track, I never was abused or tortured. I was only spanked, or, as we from the South say, I got a "whoopin'." And, being a typical boy, I deserved every whoopin' I got and didn't get as many as I deserved.

We all live in a world of rules. There are traffic rules, work rules, tax rules, and rules to live a moral life. And, as it is for all rules, if we get caught breaking one, there is some sort of price to be paid. I can think of two reasons most people don't drive as fast as they would like to. First, safety, and, second, they don't want to pay the ticket. Why don't most people rob a bank? I've never been, but I've heard that prison is rather confining. Whatever the rule is, break it and, again, if you get caught, there's usually a price to be paid.

Having said that, we break rules every day. A lot of us drive a few miles per hour over the posted speed limit or we don't completely stop at every stop sign. God's rules tell us to always tell the truth, but how many parents instruct their child to tell someone they're in the bathroom when trying to dodge an unwanted phone call? Why do we break these rules? Because we know we probably won't have to pay a cost.

When we are tempted to break a rule and we know the cost of breaking the rule, we go through a very quick process of determining the cost-to-benefit. If the cost is only a brief period of guilt, we might take the chance. As long as you know the cost, you can weigh your options. Most of us have never been to prison, but we've seen movies or read stories about prison life, so we determine that whatever we do, we don't want to do anything that will send us behind those walls.

Imagine for a second that you could actually see the prison that is hell. If it were somehow possible, if God allowed you to experience – for one twenty-four-hour period – the best, or worst, that hell has to offer, would you want to see it? Okay, I'll admit, twenty-four hours is too long. How about one hour? No? Thirty minutes, maybe? Still no? One minute, only sixty seconds. Still no? You don't even want to spend one single minute in hell? I don't blame you; nor do I.

As God-fearing Christians, none or us would volunteer to spend even one single second in hell just for the "experience." So, if we aren't willing to spend even one second in hell, what would we do to ensure that the people we love and care about don't go there? Tell them? Beg them? Now take one final step in this imaginary journey. Is there anyone who we shouldn't want to warn about the eternal danger that is hell? Has anyone ever done you so wrong or hurt you so badly that you would actually want them, from your heart, to "go to hell"?

As Jesus hung from the cross, dying for our sins, He said seven things. As He hung there in agony, both in the flesh and the spirit, one verse tells us how we are to answer the question of witnessing to the hateful and the unlovable, "Jesus said, 'Father, forgive them, for they know not what they do" (Luke 23:34a). The soldiers who nailed Jesus to the cross, the ones who mocked Him and spat upon Him, and those who were there that day, had no idea whom they were crucifying. Jesus, with what would prove to be some of His last breaths before He died His physical death, asked God not to send those responsible for His suffering to hell but to forgive them because they didn't know then what we now know.

We know that receiving a ticket for running a red light has a defined cost. You could be put into prison if you commit a felony. Stealing from work could get you fired, and cheating on a test will cost you an "F" plus get you expelled from school. Jesus told us to tell the world how they could be saved so they wouldn't have to pay the eternal cost. As Christians, our actions and words must be an example of how God wants us to live. We must tell others the cost.

Father God. I pray You would give me the words others need to hear so they will know the cost of not receiving Your free gift of eternal salvation. Amen.

And let us not grow weary in doing good, for in due season we shall reap, if we do not give up. (Galatians 6:9)

ONE MORE

Recently, I watched the movie *Hacksaw Ridge*, the World War II story of Desmond Doss, an Army medic. Due to a traumatic situation in his past, Doss swore an oath to God that he would never pick up a gun. Despite wanting to serve his country, because of that promise and his stance as a conscientious objector, his fellow soldiers branded him a coward. During the Battle of Okinawa, Doss's unit was overrun by vast numbers of Japanese infantry. Without spoiling the story, Doss, being a medic, did not abandon his fellow soldiers, choosing to remain by himself throughout the night, doing all one person could do to rescue his gravely wounded but still living brothers-in-arms.

After retrieving each wounded G.I. from the battlefield, he used a makeshift rig to lower them from the top of a cliff to fellow soldiers waiting below. Despite exhaustion and injury, after lowering a rescued soldier, Doss would look at the potentially deadly landscape and ask God to lead him to one more. "Dear Lord, let me get just one more," was Doss's constant prayer throughout the night.

Sometimes, we Christians can grow weary of doing God's work. To some, it may seem as if they are the only ones doing what they can to serve Him. That's the moment Satan will pounce and tempt us to simply quit. We age and we get tired of teaching children in Sunday school because it seems we aren't reaching anyone. We often reach the point of simply wanting to take some time off. The children we teach graduate to higher grades, and we tell ourselves it's time for other parents to take over. But God wants us to keep on, to persevere, to find just "one more."

We become discouraged because no matter how much we witness, our words seem to be falling on deaf ears or hardened hearts. We are told to bear fruit, but our tree, while full of leaves, feels empty and barren. Before long, we reach a point where we can say, "That's it. I'm done." Whenever I reach that point, I look back and remember a time, many years ago, when I was once someone's "one more." Suppose that someone, whoever that someone was, had given up on me? Would I have become a Christian? Who knows? But for whatever reason, they didn't give up.

God has never looked at me and said, "That's it. Go on, do it your way." And since God never gave up on me, I can never give up doing God's work. It's easy to choose no more; one more takes faith. Somewhere out there, your "one more" is waiting, needing you to choose to go on.

Because of Desmond Doss, 75 soldiers who probably would have otherwise perished on that hill so far from their homes survived Hacksaw Ridge. Just like Doss, when we grow tired of doing God's work, let us look to God and say, "Show me my one more."

Father God. I will admit that there are times I'm tempted to give up and let someone else do Your work. Let me not forget that somewhere there's one more out there, just waiting for me to introduce You to them. Show me my one more. Amen.

> *For if these things reside in you and abound, they ensure that you will neither be useless nor unfruitful in the knowledge of our Lord Jesus Christ.* (2 Peter 1:8)

EVER INCREASING

Most of us have heard the old business adage, "If you aren't moving forward, you're backing up." A saying from the sports world means pretty much the same thing: "Those who rest on their laurels will soon trail the race." In life, if we don't strive to be better today than we were yesterday, we'll soon look around and wonder, "Where did everyone go?"

The test you passed yesterday was great, yesterday. You need to start studying for the one you'll be having next week. You can't spend a lot of time looking in your rearview mirror to admire the first five hundred miles of your one-thousand-mile journey; you must look through the windshield to finish the next five hundred. To have a successful yesterday is fine; you should know that the world looks at you and asks, "But what have you done today?"

Peter talks about this "ever increasing" principle and how it applies to the Christian life. Beginning with faith and ending with love, Peter mentions no fewer than eight qualities we as Christians must constantly strive to increase during our daily walk with, and for, the Lord. "For this reason make every effort to add virtue to your faith; and to your virtue, knowledge; and to your knowledge, self-control; and to your self-control, patient endurance; and to your patient endurance, godliness; and to your godliness, brotherly kindness; and to your brotherly kindness, love" (2 Peter 1:5-7).

Are we constantly trying to increase our knowledge of God by reading His Word daily then applying those words in our lives? Are we exhibiting more self-control in our interactions with others in a hustle and bustle world? Do we have enough endurance to complete whatever task God gives us to do? Peter didn't say we should work on increasing one or two of these qualities; he indicated that we are to work on increasing each of them in our daily life.

By having AND increasing all these traits, we will find ourselves being both useful and fruitful in our knowledge of Jesus. Don't sit still and be satisfied with the goodness you have. Don't be satisfied with your level of godliness or brotherly affection. In the Old Testament book of Malachi, God promised this: ". . . and test Me now in this, says the Lord of Hosts, if I will not open for you the windows of heaven and pour out for you a blessing, that *there will* not *be room* enough *to receive it*" (Malachi 3:10b). If God isn't willing to stop, why should we?

Father God. Thank You for Your gift that is this life. I pray that as I read and study Your Word, You would show me the things that need increasing in my daily walk with You. Amen.

> *But the tax collector, standing at a distance, would not even lift his eyes to heaven, but struck his chest, saying, "God, be merciful to me a sinner."* (Luke 18:13)

THE OTHER R

R. A single letter out of 26. It is not the most used letter of the alphabet but certainly not the least. In just that sentence, R was used only twice while E was used 10 times and T made the most appearances with 13. While R may not be the most common letter, I happen to be fairly fond of that simple, yet important, letter. For instance, without the letter R, I would answer to the call of "Andy Glove." Now, while Andy Glove may be a fine name and I, in no way, wish to offend any or all of the Andy Gloves out there, for my sixty-plus years on this planet, I've become quite accustomed to R being the first and last letter of my name.

Many words in the English language contain the letter R; by some sources, more than 300,000. With so many R words to choose from, we Christians sometimes focus on the wrong one. A reading through the gospels tells me that Jesus wasn't too fond of a big one in some circles: Religion. He often recognized and warned against the dangers of placing one's Religion above anything else. When the goal of worship becomes making sure it is done a certain way on a certain day at a certain time to be seen by certain people (all of those things being indicative of doing Religion the RIGHT way), being Religious has become a Religion all unto itself.

If my daily goal is to read X number of Bible chapters, reading my Bible could become a Religion. If I decided attending my church would be my Religion, with its beautiful stained glass windows (I've seen none more striking), an equally beautiful sanctuary, wonderful praise and worship music, and a very insightful sermon, I could very easily do that. While it is a wonderful place to attend a church service, at its most basic, it is no more than a building. After all, Jesus had the Temple, and I'm sure it was awe-inspiring, but Jesus wanted people to know that without God, the Temple was nothing more than a really big, fancy building. But Jesus wasn't about Religion.

Jesus introduced the people to many things. He introduced the Reality – another R word – that the God of all creation, the one and only true God, the only God who is worthy of worship, could be worshipped anywhere. "For where two or three are assembled in My name, there I am in their midst" (Matthew 18:20). No, you won't find where He specifically said, "You don't have to go to Temple." He encouraged Temple attendance through His actions. Another R word He introduced was Relationship.

To the Religious leaders of Jesus' day, a direct Relationship with God was something only they could have. For common folk to think they could have a direct Relationship with God, without going through the "right" people, was the equivalent of using four-letter words from the pulpit. A direct, one-on-one Relationship with God was a foreign idea (even though there were many examples of this type of Relationship in the Old Testament) and was not advertised or welcomed by the Pharisees as something that could actually be achieved by common people. These Religious leaders encouraged – demanded, actually – the thought that a godly Relationship could only be achieved by going through the proper channels and by upholding a strict adherence to the Religious traditions of the day. When Jesus pointed out the fallacy of following that doctrine and the people (mostly "common" but not all) began to follow Him, He was seen as a threat to the power the leaders so desperately wanted to maintain.

While there is nothing inherently wrong with Religion, a Relationship with God and Jesus – true and from the heart – must be the focus of the Christian. Based on the example from Luke 18:9-14, Religion pounded its chest, threw back its head, and proudly declared, "Look at me, how great I am. I am an example for all to see." On the other hand, Relationship recognized its shortcomings and pled to the only One who could make things right: "God, have mercy on me, a sinner."

When it comes to your R's, make sure yours is the Right one.

*Heavenly Father. I thank You for the opportunity to have a loving and grateful Relationship with You and Your Son, Jesus. I know that only Your love for us and the gift of forgiveness make that Relationship possible. Let me never become so proud of my status that I would forget I am not worthy to even speak Your name. And yet, because of Your grace, mercy, and love, not only can I speak Your name, but Your name be praised.
Amen.*

> *If the whole body were an eye, where would the hearing be? If the whole body were hearing, where would the sense of smell be? But now God has established the parts, every one of them, in the body as it pleased Him. (1 Corinthians 12:17-18)*

WISHING YOU CAN

Have you ever watched someone do something and thought, "I wish I could do that"? When you thought that, most likely, you did not mean you wished you could do whatever it was that was being done. For a minute, let's say that the action being observed was a professional golfer perfectly striking a golf ball. Now, if you are given enough attempts, you could probably swing a golf club and hit a golf ball. If the truth is told, hitting a golf ball is not that hard. The hard part is making perfect contact and making that golf ball do what you want it to do. The casual golfer doesn't wish he could hit a golf ball; the casual golfer wishes he could hit a golf ball like that professional golfer. The difference between the casual golfer and the professional golfer is a little bit of talent and a whole lot of practice and dedication.

If you are a Christian, have you ever watched a preacher as he delivers his message with practiced ease? You may have envied the pianist who played their instrument, seemingly with what appears to be zero effort. How about watching someone witness to a lost person? The person doing the witnessing may make it look so natural that you find yourself wishing you could do that.

The problem with wishing for something is that we can wish and wish and wish again, but all that wishing will accomplish is . . . nothing. Wishing for the sake of wishing only makes you an accomplished wisher. Instead of wishing our lives away, we need to stop wishing and start asking God what it is He wants us to do. While you may wish that you could sing, God may want you to teach Sunday school, help usher, greet people at the church door, or serve in some other capacity in the church. And when God reveals to us what it is He wants us to do, we then must make a decision about following our wish or following His command.

Not everyone can strike a golf ball and make it bend just the right way or make it stop right beside the hole. But we can, if called upon, hold up the "Quiet Please" signs or we can count the number of people who are coming through the gate. Whatever job God may want you to do, it's up to you to join His team and do your part.

Father God. I pray I will be willing to do whatever it is You would have me do. I pray my wishes will always align with Your will for my life. Amen.

> *They are of the world, and therefore they speak from the world, and the world listens to them. We are of God, and whoever knows God listens to us. Whoever is not of God does not listen to us. This is how we know the spirit of truth and the spirit of error.* (1 John 4:5-6)

SPEAKING THE SAME LANGUAGE

According to worldatlas.com, as of December 2019, there are 195 countries in the world. And based on Ethnologue.com, for the same time period, there are 7,111 languages spoken somewhere in those countries. No matter how you count it, that's a big change from Genesis chapter 11, when everyone spoke a single language. Today, those of us who speak English can't even settle on a single variant (there's 160 different ways people speak "English"). In the South, some of us pronounce CAR by placing a heavy emphasis on the R. Drive 1,240 miles to Boston, Massachusetts and you will discover that the letter R has magically disappeared from that word. They may speak English, but, using Southern vernacular, it ain't real English.

With so many different languages, is there any way we can truly communicate? I guess it depends on how you define communicate. I had always heard that twins spoke their own language and now that I'm a grandfather of twins, I know that to be true. I'm sure you can think of a few married couples who can carry on an entire conversation with one another while only uttering a few words, if any words at all. Thanks to the people of the Shinar valley, it's been a long time since we spoke the same language. If we don't speak the same language, is it any surprise that we have so much trouble understanding each other? Can we even expect that? According to First John, no. To sum up the opening passage, people who are from the world understand the language of the world, and people who are from God understand the language of God.

When it comes to speaking the things of God, there are those who speak the truth and those who do not. Either someone is from God or they aren't. Regardless of the language, from the 1,000,000,000 people who speak Mandarin Chinese to the single Peruvian man who still speaks Taushiro, Jesus has commanded us to go to the entire world to spread the gospel.

When we spread the word, we must ensure we are speaking the truth of God. After all, when it comes to eternity, there's only one true language, the Word of God.

Father God. I pray that whenever I speak of You, You will give me the words to say so others will hear Your truth from my lips. Amen.

> *Then the king sent to him a captain of fifty with his fifty men. He went up to Elijah, and there he was, sitting on the top of a hill, and he said to him, "Man of God, the king says, 'Come down.'"* (2 Kings 1:9)

A.K.A., A MAN OF GOD

We all have a name that we answer to when called. Most of the people I know have a first name, a middle name, and a family name. I have a friend, Jackie, who has no middle name. His daddy, Freddie, had no middle name and he said, "If it's good enough for me, it's good enough for him." When Jackie's son was born, he carried on the tradition by giving his son only a first and last name. I was named after my daddy, so I am a Jr.

Some people have more than three names. I work with a man who has four, including his family name and he is a Jr. Turn to the good old Internet and you'll find out that a man – I'll call him Adolph since that's his first name – has a total of 26 names, one for each letter of the alphabet. If that's not challenging enough, his family name has a total of 666 letters. Because of the number 666, if that were my name, I probably would have been tempted to either drop or add a letter to my final name, but that's just me.

A lot of us answer to nicknames. All of my life I have answered to Randy (except when Momma was mad, then she would call me by all of my names, including Jr.). My given name is Randolph, so Randy is my nickname. There are others who answer to either their initials or to a name that came from either their physical shape, something they did, or was just formulated out of thin air. I work with the following group of people: Tadpole, Wimp, Cheese, Bubba, Koolaid, Jersey, Slim, Tiny, Jughead, Bozo, Corndog, Butters, and Red. I'm sure I forgot some, but you get the picture. Regardless of what we are called, each name – to us – is significant.

The Bible doesn't really give us many nicknames. If it did, Job might have answered to Toughy because of his run of suspected bad luck. But it does give us instances when people were called by something other than their real name. In the book of Second Kings, we hear some young boys calling Elisha old baldhead. After 42 of those boys were torn to pieces by two bears, I would imagine word quickly spread that Elisha didn't care for that nickname.

Earlier in the same book, Elijah was referred to as "Man of God." It must have been so because after he had been called that, God's presence within Elijah was evident. "But Elijah answered the captain of fifty: 'If I am a man of God, then let fire come down from heaven and consume you and your fifty men.' Then fire came down from heaven and consumed him and his fifty men" (2 Kings 1:10). After this had happened a second time, the third captain sent to Elijah developed a plan. "Then again the king sent a third captain of fifty with his fifty men. The third captain of fifty went up, came and fell on his knees before Elijah, and pleaded with him, 'Man of God, may my life and the life of these fifty servants of yours be precious in your sight'" (2 Kings 1:13).

It is said we are known by the company we keep. We are called by a name we were given or one we earned. Elijah was called a man of God and it's obvious the name fit. If our life reflects our belief, could we answer to the name, man – or woman – of God? If it doesn't, we may need to work on that.

Father God. I'm not sure what You will call me when I get to heaven. I'm just thankful I will be there to hear the name You've picked for me. Amen.

> *There is one body and one Spirit, even as you were called in one hope of your calling, one Lord, one faith, one baptism, one God and Father of all, who is above all, and through all, and in you all.* (Ephesians 4:4-6)

CAT SKINNIN'

Being a lifelong Southerner, I've heard many old sayings that apply to the various situations we face in our modern life. The two sayings, "When you find your hole getting deeper, stop digging," and "You made your bed, lie in it," both apply when we find ourselves in some sort of trouble that we had a hand in making. Then there are other sayings that make me scratch my head. One that I've heard for years, "There's more than one way to skin a cat," makes me wonder how that affirmation originated. Now that I think about it, I probably don't want to know. If it has anything to do with cats, I certainly wouldn't want to have been that cat. Whatever the case may be, those words can certainly be applied to more activities than cat skinnin'.

If an inventor sees a better way to build something, he may not think about it this way, but he's skinnin' cats. When Paula Dean comes up with a brand-spanking-new way to make some delectable dessert, she's skinnin' cats. When I was a young lad cutting two acres of grass with a 20-inch push mower, I know one of the zero-turn, 60-inch mowers of our modern life would have been a better way to skin that particular cat. Everywhere we turn, there are improvements in practically all aspects of 21st century life. Whether one is cooking, cleaning, painting, studying, or shaving, whatever the activity, there are now more choices to do practically anything that needs doing. Even for Christians, we have several ways we can worship and learn about God.

All of that being said, when it comes to the actual act of salvation, Jesus made it as plain as day that there is but a single way one can be saved. After being asked by Thomas, one of His disciples, how they would know the way, "Jesus said to him, 'I am the way, the truth, and the life. No one comes to the Father except through Me'" (John 14:6).

If you are looking for another way to receive salvation, you can try to find it by reading that verse in other versions of the Bible. You can hear or watch church services in person, on television, radio, or on the Internet. Yes, you can hear about Jesus and God and salvation nearly as many ways as you can imagine skinnin' a cat. But when it comes to attaining eternal salvation, believe me when I tell you this: There's only one way to skin that cat. And that's the Jesus way.

Dear Jesus. Thank You for telling us exactly what we must do in order to receive Your gift of eternal forgiveness and salvation. Amen.

Therefore be perfect, even as your Father who is in heaven is perfect. (Matthew 5:48)

ON TARGET

Nobody's perfect. Despite the claim, we have turned those two words into the perfect excuse. If excuses were cards to be played, "nobody's perfect" is the all-purpose card that can be presented each and every time we mess up. Took a wrong turn down a one-way street? Nobody's a perfect driver. Overcooked the Thanksgiving turkey? Nobody's a perfect cook. Forget to pay a utility bill? Nobody's . . . well, you know the rest. Since Adam, Eve, the serpent, and that tree in the middle of the garden, other than Jesus, I can't think of a single soul who never has used that excuse.

Perfection. No, I'm not talking about a fictitious small Nevada town that has some pre-historic worms that tunnel around and terrorize the locals. If you saw the movie *Tremors*, that sentence makes perfect sense. The perfection I'm talking about is defined in the dictionary as having the highest degree of proficiency, skill, or excellence or it is the state or quality of being or becoming perfect. And there are times we, as humans, can achieve that most rare of states. Sport fans can think of the perfect pass, perfectly striking a golf ball, or a baseball pitcher having a perfect game.

But how about spiritual perfection? Can any of us ever achieve, or even hope to achieve, spiritual perfection? For anyone old enough to know the difference between right and wrong, sadly, the answer to that question is no. Once we sin, that is we willfully do something that we know God doesn't want us to do, we have permanently erased our chance at a perfectly sinless life. The Bible tells us this in Romans: "For all have sinned and come short of the glory of God" (Romans 3:23). The cost for our spiritual imperfection? Death and eternal separation from God. "For the wages of sin is death" (Romans 6:23a) and, "No unclean thing shall ever enter it [heaven], nor shall anyone who commits abomination or falsehood" (Revelation 21:27a). So, if we all are going to sin and no one who sins has a chance to get into heaven, why should we even attempt perfection?

There are moments that we do the perfect thing, that thing that God would have us do in whatever situation we find ourselves. When we tell the whole truth when it would have been easier to tell a lie. We return the money when someone gives us too much change. We make an honest B- instead of cheating to get the A. These, and countless other moments are what we must strive to do on a daily basis. Why? Because our goal is not behind us but lies at the end of this road we call life. Paul tells us this when he reminds us, "I press toward the goal to the prize of the high calling of God in Christ Jesus" (Philippians 3:14).

If we can't remain spiritually perfect, how can we get into heaven? While we all sin and sin equals death and no one with sin can enter heaven, we can all take heart in these two passages: ". . . but the gift of God is eternal life through Jesus Christ our Lord" (Romans 6:23b) and ". . . but only those whose names are written in the Lamb's Book of Life [will enter heaven]" (Revelation 21:27b).

Archers and marksmen aim for perfection. Students should desire perfect grades. Golfers want the hole-in-one. Christians? Even though no one is perfect, we must remember that our daily aim should be to please the One who gave us our perfect forgiveness.

Lord Jesus. May I remember every day that You are the reason that I have been perfectly forgiven of my many imperfections. I thank You for that forgiveness and I pray I would never take it for granted. Amen.

R.G. Glover

If we confess our sins, He is faithful and just to forgive us our sins and cleanse us from all unrighteousness. (1 John 1:9)

YOUR FILTER

Filtration: the ability to remove impurities or other unwanted or undesirable elements from a base material. Your vehicle's engine not only has fuel, oil, and air filters but most modern vehicles have an interior cabin air filter. At home, I filter the water that I and my dogs drink (yep, they're spoiled), my refrigerator makes ice from filtered water, and I have three air filters for the air I breathe. Respirators provide safe air for those working in environments having hazardous atmospheres. Modern coffeepots not only filter the grounds but they often have additional water filters (I forgot about that one). If we could see inside us, we would find a liver, two lungs, a nose, two kidneys, and other organs that filter out the bad things that find their way into our bodies.

For a filter to earn the High Efficiency Particulate Air (HEPA) certification, it must be capable of filtering 99.97% of all particles that are larger than 0.03 microns in size. If you didn't know, 0.03 microns is real tiny. If the filter can't do that, it may be a good filter but, as we Southerners say, it ain't a HEPA filter. But even HEPA filters won't guarantee that they filter 100% of all particles, regardless of how small they are. Suppose your heavenly eternity depended on your being 100% sin-free (and it does), would you be willing to settle for 99.97%? HEPA filters are great for vacuuming and air filtration, but to get to heaven, we must remove 100% of the sin from our life.

When God determined the rule to get into heaven, He didn't say that those who were cleaned of all but 0.03% of their sin would be okay. What He said was none. God said no sin. Since none of us are totally sin-free, that's a problem. We either must be 100% sinless or 100% forgiven, and, since we aren't sinless, we must be forgiven. We're going to have to rely on the perfect sin filter that is the blood and salvation of Jesus to enter heaven.

Eventually, every filter we buy must be replaced. They can only filter so much before they become ineffective. Fortunately for us, our sin filter costs nothing, it never wears out, and it never needs replacement. Do you have sin in your life? What you need is a Jesus filter.

Lord Jesus. Thank You for filtering the sin from my life. I pray that anyone who has not asked for their cleansing would find it in their heart to take care of that problem before it's too late. Amen.

The mountains melt like wax at the presence of the Lord, at the presence of the Lord of the earth. (Psalm 97:5)

OVERCOMING MOUNTAINS

Everest. K2. Denali. The Matterhorn. Kilimanjaro. Fuji. Mauna Lea. Cheaha. Have you ever seen any of these or any other mountain? Rising from the earth, these majestic peaks beg us to reach for the skies. Some are higher than others. As far as mountain climbing goes, Mt. Cheaha, the highest peak in Alabama, isn't a big deal. And while I didn't climb the entire 2,413 feet above sea level to reach Mt. Cheaha's summit, I have stood on that summit. But even as he stood on that summit, the boy that was me wondered what it would be like to stand on top of the world.

Mt. Everest, at 29,029 feet above sea level, is the highest mountain on earth. I've seen pictures of it and watched documentaries of people who have scaled to the very summit of the earth. While books have been written about those who survived the arduous climb, there are also stories of those who remain on the frozen slopes. Overcome by the elements or falling to their ultimate demise, they never returned from what would surely have been the epitome of their climbing life.

When some were asked why they wanted to attempt something from which they could very well not return, their answer was, "Because it's there." Most of us will never know the struggle of the climb or experience the exhilaration of standing on the summit. But we all have our own personal summits we must conquer. What started out as a strange-looking mole or a small cough could turn into a life-altering disease. The big house with a pool, nice cars, and credit cards were manageable until the dream job fell apart and now you dread answering the phone, weary of talking to creditors. Your promise of, "I'll have just one drink," has long since passed and now you have to find a way home. The drug that your friends said is "no big deal" now has you firmly in its grasp. The parents who raised you from birth are now aging and need your care.

Not every problem is huge. Shoestrings break, the baby spills its food, the power goes out, or the tire goes flat – at night – in the rain –

and you're late for your anniversary dinner. No matter the problem, we all struggle from time to time. Every problem won't be Mt. Everest, but every problem must be overcome.

In Matthew 17:20, Jesus said if we had the faith of a mustard seed, we could move mountains. We may never have to move a mountain, but when our small hills become towering obstacles, let us first seek God before whom the mountains melt.

Father God. Let me remember that problems, while seemingly like mountains, are found in every life. Remind me to trust You so the mountains in my life will be smoothed out so I can travel the path You have made for me. Amen.

> *The Lord is not slow concerning His promise, as some count slowness. But He is patient with us, because He does not want any to perish, but all to come to repentance.* (2 Peter 3:9)

A ONE-SIZE GOD

One size fits all. Being a guy who likes to fish, who used to play a good bit of golf, and who follows Alabama football and NASCAR, I own several pieces of headgear (i.e., caps). Two of them are fitted to my particular head size, but most of them are adjustable, the idea being they can fit a fairly wide range of head sizes. If you look on the inside of those caps, you will find a label that proclaims, "One Size Fits Most." How times have changed. That same label used to read, "One Size Fits All." I guess a cap manufacturer was sued because their cap didn't fit a particular head. Anyway, the manufacturers of those caps are telling any who will listen that their cap, once properly adjusted, can be made to fit practically every head on the face of the planet. I have found that, although I can adjust a lot of caps to be the right size for my head, not every cap "fits" my head. The circumference may be correct, but the feel often isn't.

In our world, life is like those caps. We adjust our car seats until they are just right. We adjust the water temperature so our shower isn't too hot or too cold. Too much or too little seasoning and we have a meal that, while edible, isn't quite what we want. A mattress can appear to be perfect until we lie on it. The beach is a wonderful place for some, but not everyone likes crowds, sand, humidity, and scorching sun. Let's face it, the claim "one size fits all" isn't always true.

Suppose God's gift of salvation came with a size label. If we read that label and it claimed that one dose of this forgiveness elixir would erase [enter the number here] sins, how many sins would you need forgiven? You would want to make sure you were covered. But, in the fine print, you read that you only get one shot at this and you can't enter a number too high; it has to be exactly the number of sins you have committed, and it must include those you have yet to commit. Hmmm.

Fortunately for us, or at least for me, God's gift doesn't come with an expiration label or a size limit. God is a one-size fits all God for all time. He forgives all of our sin, no matter how severe and no matter how many. There is no sin that is too great for God's forgiveness. If you've committed only one or you just clicked off sin number 1,000,000,000,000,000 (wow, that's a lotta sin; you've been busy), God tells us He is faithful to forgive every one of them.

Once, while doing some shopping at a NASCAR race, I tried on a cap that bore the image of my favorite driver (Go Wowdy!). I really liked the way it looked but, although I tried, I never could quite get it to fit. I put it back on the rack and walked away, thinking, "Too bad it only fits most." I may have missed out on that cap but, because God's forgiveness is "One Dose Forgives All," I know I won't miss my heavenly destination.

Lord Jesus. Thank You for Your gift of eternal salvation that covers all of my sins, no matter how big or how many. Thank You for being a one-sized Savior. Amen.

> *Out of all these people there were seven hundred specially chosen men who were left-handed, all of whom could sling a stone at a hair and not miss.* (Judges 20:16)

ONE SINGLE DEGREE

Each of us have targets in our lives that we must hit to be successful in whatever endeavor we attempt. Let's say it is possible to walk around the entire earth along the equator. Your target is to walk around the entire planet, ending your trip precisely where it began. You must circle the globe, walking in an easterly direction, until you have covered the entire 24,901 miles; all the while remembering your goal of stopping exactly where you began.

And so you begin. Paraphrasing the Chinese proverb, you take the first step of a multi-thousand-mile journey. You align yourself and, as we say in the South, "commence to walking." After thousands of hours, you take the final step of the trip, completing the entire 24,901 miles. There's only one problem. You are nowhere near your starting point. As you recount your trip, you learn that you were off course by one degree north of due east during the entire walk. That error of one degree resulted in you being 433.8 miles north of your intended destination. Let's say you try again, but this time, you discover you were only $1/10^{th}$ of one degree off course. Will that matter? Not really, if you don't mind missing your mark by just 43.38 miles.

Being off target causes many people to wander through life wondering why they never seem to hit the mark. If NASA had been a single degree off target when Apollo 11 left Cape Canaveral with its target being the moon's Sea of Tranquility, they would have only missed their target (the moon) by a little more than 4,000 miles. Would 4,000 miles have been enough to abort the mission? Probably not. Course corrections are routinely made during any flight, including space flight. And by making many course corrections during the flight, instead of hearing Buzz Aldrin say, "Uhhhhh, Houston," we were able to hear Neil Armstrong from the surface of the moon, "Houston, Tranquility Base here. The Eagle has landed."

What is your target? For the Christian, according to Matthew 5:48, our target is perfection. And let us imagine that, for a period, we are hitting our target. We love all, including our enemies. We live exactly as the Bible tells us we should live. As time goes on, by committing the occasional "minor" sin, we begin to stray slightly to the left or to the right. Not realizing we are off course, we continue to live our life without making a single course correction. When we arrive at the end of our life's journey, we look around, expecting to be greeted by, as some would believe, St. Peter standing at the pearly gates. But, because we assumed we were being fairly perfect and we did not ask God for forgiveness of our sins, we never made the necessary correction in our course. We missed our target.

Missing a trashcan when you toss a wad of paper is no big deal. Missing a turn as you drive to work might make you late, but it's not the end of the world. The kicker that misses the game winning, come-from-behind, field goal may lose his starting job, but he can start over and do better. Because of our sinful nature, we usually miss our goal of perfection. God will correct our course, but we must seek Him out.

Dear God. Thank You for giving me a way to correct my course and hit my target.
Amen.

> *Nevertheless do not rejoice that the spirits are subject to you, but rather rejoice that your names are written in heaven.*
> (Luke 10:20)

NON-SMUDGING INK

As I grow older, I find myself appreciating things that, at one time, I was quick to take for granted. For instance, because I never leave my house without one, I appreciate a good writing ink pen, particularly those with gel-based inks. There was a time when ballpoint pens, although they were better suited for a modern, more portable society than fountain pens, had an irritating fault. When you made a line with them, the ink would, for lack of a better description, "glob up." After making a line, you would have to wipe the pen's tip with a paper towel or a napkin before any further use.

Although many of the gel ink pens no longer exhibit that nasty trait, there are still some that require you to allow the ink to dry for a few seconds. If you don't do this, you'll find yourself with a smeared signature and ink on your hand or fingers. Because of some really smart people, I can now find pens that have ink that dries practically the second the ball leaves the paper. But when it comes to smudging, even gel-based ink has its limitations. Shiny paper and other surfaces don't absorb the ink and, if you need to write on those surfaces, you'll need some type of permanent ink marker. Even then, depending on the writing surface, drying time is still required to prevent smudging.

The Bible mentions writing in several places. Paul tells us that he writes "in his hand," and, in Revelation, John was instructed to both "write what he had seen" and "do not write what he had seen." We know the Bible is the written Word of God as recorded by men who were inspired by God. With all of the writing that is the Bible, there is a specifically mentioned book that has writing that directly affects the life of every person.

When someone accepts Jesus as their Lord and Savior and they are adopted into God's family, their names are recorded in the Lamb's Book of Life. Although the specific type of ink is not mentioned, it seems logical that our names are written with the ink that doesn't smudge and never fades. If it is through the blood of Jesus that we are saved, logic tells me that the very same blood is the ink that wrote each of our names in that book.

The same blood that washes away my sin and cleans me as white as newly driven snow is the ink that guarantees my eternity with the One who shed it. While a gel-based ink pen may make a decent writing instrument, the blood of Jesus is the only truly non-smudging ink.

Lord Jesus. Thank You for shedding the blood that saved me from my sins. I thank You for writing my name in Your book of life. And I thank You for the heavenly home I will share with all others whose names are written in the same book. Amen.

> *Then Jesus said to him, "Get away from here, Satan! For it is written, 'You shall worship the Lord your God, and Him only shall you serve.' Then the devil left Him, and immediately angels came and ministered to Him."* (Matthew 4:10-11)

THE MASTER MANIPULATOR

Have you ever been associated with someone who could have the descriptive "Manipulator" on their business card? When you add political motivation to the COVID-19 crisis we are currently experiencing, if pressed for a name, I'm sure we can all identify several political "leaders" who fit this description. In my personal life, I have been associated with a small number of people who would always, and I mean *always*, try to manipulate whatever situation they found themselves in or whomever they happened to be with at the moment.

In life, we all manipulate things from time to time. We adjust water temperature for the perfect shower or bath, we season food so it tastes like we like, or we arrange furniture so it will best suit the room. When it comes to manipulating people, the dictionary definition would be to influence or manage shrewdly or deviously. If I had written that definition, I would describe a manipulator as someone who is "in it to win it." The manipulator's goal is to win at any cost.

A manipulator will immediately determine if someone is a threat or if they can use someone as a means to an end. As I said earlier, I have known a few of these people. Because I don't approve of their methods, I only associate with them when absolutely necessary. There are those at our workplaces who are said to be looking for a place to stick a figurative knife when they pat you on the back. Whether it be work, school, or even family, whatever the situation or the relationship, each of us knows a manipulator who puts all others to shame.

Satan, the Master Manipulator, wants to use us to attack God. When we slip up and sin, he will tell any and all that we may claim to be a Christian, but we are nothing more than a fraud. Satan tried that trick with Jesus. In the fourth chapter of Matthew, we read that Jesus was led into the desert to be tempted by the devil. After forty days and nights of fasting, Jesus was hungry. Satan, sensing an opportunity, jumped from his hiding place. "If You are the Son of God, command that these stones be turned into bread" (Matthew 4:3b). I don't know about you, but if I were that hungry and as much as I like bread, that would have been a strong temptation to resist. But not Jesus. He turned to Satan, His one-time heavenly friend, and told him we do not live by bread alone, ". . . but by every word that proceeds out of the mouth of God" (Matthew 4:4b).

The Bible tells of other times Satan tried to tempt Jesus. I would imagine that Satan tried to tempt Jesus to avoid His death on the cross. Matthew's gospel tells us how Jesus handled Satan's manipulation, "He went a little farther, and falling on His face, He prayed, 'O My Father, if it is possible, let this cup pass from me," and later, "He went away a second time and prayed, 'O My Father, if this cup cannot pass away from Me unless I drink it, Your will be done" (Matthew 26:39a, 42). For every temptation Satan threw, Jesus countered with His will to obey God and to resist the devil.

The next time we face a manipulator, remember what Jesus did. Resist the flattery and the temptation and do what we know is right.

My Lord and Savior, Jesus. I know that You have faced temptations that I pray I never have to face. But, if it comes down to it, I pray that You would give me the strength to face it as You would, obedient to the end. Amen.

> *For you shall not go out with haste nor go by flight. For the Lord will go before you, and the God of Israel will be your rear guard.* (Isaiah 52:12)

GOD HAS YOUR BACK

Watch your six, protect your blindside, or cover your rear flank. There are many ways to say it, but you must always protect yourself from an opponent who will, if given the slightest opportunity, hit you when and where you are least expecting it, that place usually being from somewhere behind you. While we can become so busy watching where we are going, the devil, being a master of ambush, is sneaking up behind us, always looking for the chance to pounce.

The 2009 movie, *The Blind Side*, was about Michael Oher, a large, black, homeless, young man who would eventually find not one, but two homes. His internal crisis of not having a family was solved when he was adopted by a white family who truly loved and cared for him as a person. He found his other home on the green grass of a football field.

Because of his impressive physical size and ability, Michael discovered that he was a natural offensive tackle, and not just any tackle, but a left tackle. For the right-handed quarterback, the left tackle is the guy who will be protecting the side you don't normally see, your blind side. The right-handed quarterback always depends on his left tackle having his back.

In the world of aerial combat, the pilot who can attack from the rear has the advantage. Knowing this, the designers of World War II bombers included a rear-facing gun turret. The young man who crawled into that pod had one job, to protect the plane from enemy fighters who were zooming in to attack from the rear. He protected the plane's blind side.

The seminal story in the Old Testament, the Hebrew exodus from Egypt, tells of the importance God placed on protecting Israel's blind side as they fled Pharaoh. "Then the angel of God, which went before the camp of Israel, moved and went behind them, and the pillar of the cloud moved before them and stood behind them. So it came between the camp of the Egyptians and the camp of Israel" (Exodus 14:19-20a). God, who was preparing to part the Red Sea so the Israelites could escape the wrath of the Egyptian king, sent His protection to the rear of the Hebrew people, blocking the attack of the Egyptian army.

God knows that our enemy, Satan, will stop at no point in his daily attacks. We can't always see a full 360° around us. Somewhere, there is an opening in our defense. We have to have our parent's "eyes in the back of our heads," but that set of eyes doesn't belong to our mom or dad. Those eyes belong to our heavenly Father. Those are the eyes of God, and God has our back.

Eternal Father. I pray that You will continue to watch all around me as You block the charges of my ancient enemy, Satan. I thank You for the protection You give me throughout my day and night. Amen.

The king answered and said to the man of God, "Seek the face of the Lord your God, and pray for me, that my hand will be healed." And the man of God interceded with the Lord, and the king's hand was healed and became as it was before.
(1 Kings 13:6)

BEING UNKNOWN

Several years ago, the National Football League's New Orleans Saints franchise were a far cry from the team they have become. They were routinely one of the worst teams in the NFL. Whenever another team found the Saints on their schedule, they could normally count that game as a victory, even to the point of planning on playing some of the players who would not normally have an opportunity to play.

While all teams struggle from time-to-time, the Saints redefined the meaning of the word *struggle*. They performed so poorly that some of their fans would wear paper bags over their heads as they sat in the stands, not wanting to be identified as Saints fans. While those Saints fans of years gone by may have been famous for being unknown, modern day Saints fans, with their jerseys and shouts of "Who Dat?" are anything but unknown.

When you perform a task, is it important that you be recognized by name? There's an old saying that goes something like this, "It's amazing what can be accomplished when no one cares who gets the credit." While reading the Bible, if you read the 13th chapter of the book of 1 Kings, you will find a man identified only as "a man of God." Depending on the version of the Bible you read, you may find the "man of God" mentioned up to sixteen times but nowhere will you find his actual name. He even answers to that phrase as if it is his actual name: "He went after the man of God and found him sitting under an oak, and he said to him, 'Are you the man of God who came from Judah?' And he said, 'I am'" (1 Kings 13:14).

Is it important that people remember the things we do? Perhaps. Is it important that we are remembered because we served God? Without a doubt, yes! I appreciate that those paper-bag-wearing Saints fans were at the game, but why be a part of something if you are ashamed of it? If you're proud to be a part of God's team, let the world know. One thing the world doesn't need is unknown Christians.

Eternal God. Thank You for adopting me into Your family so I could be called Your child. I pray that I won't let my pride get in the way of doing Your works here on earth and I look forward to an eternity in heaven in my future. Amen.

> *This Book of the Law must not depart from your mouth. Meditate on it day and night so that you may act carefully according to all that is written in it. For then you will make your way successful, and you will be wise.* (Joshua 1:8)

JUST THE MINIMUM

A friend of mine once had a belief that some people made it through life with a condition his wife called MWM, or minimum wage mentality. In her opinion, those people approached everything they did with the state of mind that says, "I make the minimum, so I do the minimum." I will admit, I know some people who wallow through life with that mentality. They show up just before they are late and they go about their day doing just their job; nothing more, often something less.

I've tried to help some of them. What I try to show those people, if they will allow me, is that getting a job is just the start. When I ask them what it would take for them to put forth more effort, I sometimes hear this answer, "If they would pay me more, I would work harder." I try to remind them that life doesn't function that way, at least in the business world. In the business world, if you want to earn more, you have to show the boss that you are worthy of more.

There are some Christians who treat their study of God's Word with the same attitude. If the only verse you can quote with any confidence is the old standby, "For God so loved the world that He gave His only begotten Son, that whoever believes in Him should not perish, but have eternal life" (John 3:16), you've not done a whole lot of Bible study. If you're like me, you were taught that verse from the King James Version of the Bible (remember whosoever, believeth, and everlasting?). Regardless of the version, if you've only read that single verse, that's pretty much the minimum.

Jesus never told us it would be good enough to just rest on our faith. Nowhere in the Bible will you read that either God or His Son told us they only expect the minimum. If that were true, why did Jesus have the expectation that we would spread the good news throughout the world?

Yes, faith is what it takes to be saved, but being saved is just the beginning. If you seek shelter from a storm, are you satisfied with just stepping across the threshold or do you jump all the way in? John 3:16 is a wonderful verse, but it's only a single verse. I'm sure you don't want a "just the minimum" Savior. If you could ask Him, I'm also sure Jesus doesn't want "just the minimum" Christians.

> *Eternal Savior. I thank You for the eternal words of hope that are found on every page of the Bible. I pray that instead of the minimum, You would show me the maximum of what You expect and that I would be willing to give You my maximum effort. Amen.*

> *What man among you having a hundred sheep and losing one of them does not leave the ninety-nine in the wilderness and go after the one which is lost until he finds it?* (Luke 15:4)

THE MISSING PIECE

How I used to enjoy putting jigsaw puzzles together. Regardless of the number of pieces, anywhere from one hundred to multiple thousands, placing that final piece of the jigsaw puzzle always gave me a sense of accomplishment. I can remember, years ago, when my mother and I would open a new puzzle box, empty the pieces on a card table, turn them all face up, and, starting with the edge pieces, begin snapping the pieces together to form what would eventually become a picture.

Bubba, my dad's mother, also enjoyed her jigsaw puzzles. With a house full of men and boys (her husband and their four sons), the entire family would pitch in to help. Because someone in that group always wanted to be the one who completed the puzzle, one or two pieces would usually be missing when the end was near. When no one was looking, that final piece would miraculously be found and somehow make its way to its designated spot, finally completing the puzzle.

If you've ever worked for several hours, or, in some cases, days on a jigsaw puzzle only to discover a piece missing, you feel as if you've worked for nothing. You could just look at the nearly-completed puzzle, appreciate your effort, sigh deeply, shrug your shoulders, tear it apart, put it back into the box, mark it up as experience, and go on to your next challenge. You could do that, but if you are like me, you won't. Sure, you've put together 999 pieces but all you can concentrate on is finding that $1,000^{th}$ piece. You're not going to stop looking; even if it means turning the whole house upside down, you're bound and determined to find that missing piece. Some would tell you, "Good job. Look what you accomplished. Look, it's just a puzzle, it's not the end of the world." Thanks for the encouragement, but all I see is that small hole where that missing piece should be, so I continue to look until it's found.

Jesus tells a story about searching for that which was lost when He gave an account of a shepherd searching for a single missing sheep.

Some would have been happy with the ninety-nine that remained, but that shepherd searched until he found that single lost sheep. "And when he has found it, he places it on his shoulders, rejoicing. Then when he comes home, he calls together his friends and neighbors, saying to them, 'Rejoice with me, for I have found my sheep which was lost'" (Luke 15:5-6).

Yes, in the end, a jigsaw puzzle is just a jigsaw puzzle, missing piece or not. But, as Christians, we are told to look for the lost so they can be found. What about the one who "found" Bubba's missing puzzle piece? There was usually a price to be paid. But that price is mild when compared to the eternal price for the lost person who is never found.

My Lord and Savior. Thank You for the ones who led me to You so I would be among those who were found by You. I pray I am willing to help someone who is lost so I could lead them to You.
Amen.

> *The famine was over all the face of the earth, so Joseph opened all the storehouses and sold to the Egyptians, and the famine was severe throughout the land of Egypt.* (Genesis 41:56)

YOUR STOREHOUSE

Ask any farmer and you will quickly discover that good weather is for planting, caring for, and harvesting the crops that were planted. It is during the calm between storms that crops are harvested and storehouses filled. Every farmer worth his salt understands that for every good day, bad days cannot be far off, waiting somewhere just beyond the horizon. Wasting a day to gather is setting yourself up for difficulty in the future. As farming goes, spring, summer, and fall are for growing the hay then putting it in the barn, for winter will surely come and cows can't eat hay that was never grown, cut, loaded on the wagon, and stacked to the ceiling.

The Christian life is like the farmer. As we breeze through life's good times, we need to make sure we are growing and storing our faith. God begins by giving us seeds of faith. That faith is nurtured by daily Bible reading. Daily prayer fertilizes that faith so it will grow. Good days, days that are overflowing with God's blessings, are days for strengthening and storing our faith. Our faith storehouse can never have enough.

Then there are days when we must draw on our stored faith. You lose your job, time to make a faith withdrawal. An unexpected financial need jumps up, dip into your faith account. You receive a bad medical report and now your future is uncertain, lots of faith is now needed. Your parents travel the last part of their road of life – that same path we all must one day face – having a storehouse full of faith will be a blessing. Times like those will test the faith we have stored. If you haven't gathered and nurtured your faith crop, you will find those times may be more than you can take.

Storms come in every life, some more than others. Dark days lead to darker nights. Those are the times you could curl up and fear the times to come or you could kneel and see the promise of better times in the future.

Yes, we must rest during our faith harvest. God gave us that example, but we must never allow our faith crop to wither from inattention. The people of Egypt and surrounding areas would have starved if Joseph had not listened to God and built storehouses for food. God gave us the seed of faith we need. It's our job to make sure that faith is there when the drought comes.

Lord and God. Thank You for the seeds of faith You give each of us. Let us not waste our crop through inattention or indifference. Provide for me a storehouse so I can store the faith I will need in the days to come. Amen.

Whom [Jesus Christ], having not seen, you love; and in whom, though you do not see Him now, you believe and you rejoice with joy unspeakable and full of glory, receiving as the result of your faith the salvation of your souls. (1 Peter 1:8-9)

LOVING THE UNSEEN

Parents are a strange bunch. We do things for our children that we would do for no one else. We love our children in a way that was unfathomable before they were born. We may not approve of everything they do, but our love for them knows no end. For a minute, if you have children, think back to the very first time you found out you were going to be a parent. I remember hearing the words, "We're going to have a baby!"

At first, excitement, "Wow! I'm going to be a daddy!" Then, reality, "I'm going to be a daddy? I don't know nothing about being a daddy. What in the world? Whew. . ." After my initial excitement, it dawned on me that I truly didn't know what I didn't know. I was going to be a daddy. Talk about an emotional roller coaster. I didn't know anything about being a daddy, but I did know one thing. Before she was even a bump in my wife's belly, long before we found out that she would be a she, I loved that little person to be. I had no idea what she would look like, and I hadn't even heard one little whimper of a cry, but I knew that she had me wrapped around her little finger.

For pretty much any Christian that has ever lived, we are to feel the same way about Jesus. To my knowledge, I've never seen Christ. I don't know how tall He is or how much He weighs. I don't know the pitch of His voice or the texture of His hands. His shoe size is a mystery as is His favorite meal. I don't think He has tattoos, but I do know He has body piercings. I don't know what I don't know, but I do know I love Him and He loves me. With Him, I feel a love and a peace that are beyond comprehension. Just as I would do whatever I could for my daughter, I know He will do whatever it takes to get me through this life.

Now that Heather is grown and has babies of her own (twins, boy and girl), I see a woman that at one time was just a twinkle in my eye. My love for her has only grown over time. What's the difference between Jesus and me? Until I learned that I was going to be a daddy, I had no idea my daughter would ever exist. Jesus, on the other hand, knew about me when He hung on that cross. He's loved me when I've done exactly what He wanted, and He's loved me when I couldn't have been farther from who He wanted me to be.

There was a time I couldn't imagine loving someone like I love my daughter. And I can't imagine how it will feel when, at last, I finally see the One who died for me so that one day I could live with Him.

Lord Jesus. Thank You for the gift that is my daughter. And I thank You for the gift that is my salvation. I know I deserved neither, but You have given me both. I look forward to the day when I, the un-loveable, get to see You, the source of all that is love. Amen.

> *Live your lives honorably among the Gentiles, so that though they speak against you as evildoers, they shall see your good works and thereby glorify God in the day of visitation.*
> (1 Peter 2:12)

THE NEXT TIME

My job has presented me the opportunity to attend lots of training, both within and outside my company. Much of my training has taken place at two respected universities: Georgia Tech University in Atlanta, Georgia and the University of Alabama in Tuscaloosa, Alabama. While attending training, I have sat through classes with many instructors. All of those instructors were very knowledgeable about the subject matter, but each of them had their own individual teaching styles.

One particular instructor was, by all accounts, a very smart man. He was a full-time professor at another university, and he had a bunch of letters behind his name on his business card that indicated he had attended a lot of school, passed a lot of tests, and spent a lot of money on both. As smart as he was, over the years, he had developed a bad habit, especially for someone whose job it is to talk for a living. As he would speak, he would constantly use two of what are known as "crutch" words: "Okay" and "K." How many times is constant? During one fifty-minute session, he used those words 139 times. Yes, I counted.

Fast forward to today. I recently attended a meeting led by one of our younger engineers. He is very smart but his crutch word, as with many of the youth of today, was "like." He described a new computer software system that, "Like, when it is, like, installed, in our, like, remote, like, locations, it will, like, record all of the, like, voltage demands on, like, the system." And no, like, I'm not, like, exaggerating. Okay? Sorry, I couldn't resist.

Whenever I am listening to someone speak and they begin to use crutch words, I find myself missing the content because I am listening for the next "like" or "okay" or whatever word they use (one of my workmates likes the word "Cool"). It can be like that when someone claiming to be a Christian uses words or does things that indicate that person is anything but Christian.

When someone proclaims to the world that they are Christian, the world starts looking for opportunities to point out any "other than Christian" words and behaviors. When we willfully sin, our witness for the world will quickly overshadow our witness for the Gospel. While Christians are in no way perfect, our goal must be to show the world that we live and speak for Christ.

Whenever I stand in front of an audience talking about different topics, I have to remind myself that, because I don't want someone waiting for my next "okay" or "like," I must avoid using words that can distract from my main point. And when it comes to my Christian walk, I must remember that someone is out there waiting for the next time I will, like, slip or, like, fall. Okay?

Eternal Savior. I pray You would guard my words and my actions so others will see and hear You through the life I live.
Amen.

> *The Lord is good to those who wait for Him, to the soul who seeks Him. It is good that a man should wait quietly for the salvation of the Lord.* (Lamentations 3:25-26)

ONCE IN A LIFETIME

As far back as I can remember, I have been fascinated with space. I can remember looking into a summer's night sky and thinking, "I wonder . . ." For a young boy who grew up during the race to the moon, many things in space held a certain fascination. I remember watching the moon landing on a small black and white television and hearing Neil Armstrong's voice through the speaker as his foot first touched the moon's dusty surface, "That's one small step for man." When I hear Sputnik, I don't say, "Huh? What?" I saw Haley's comet during its most recent passage near our planet. Many of us remember Columbia, Challenger, Apollo 1, and Apollo 13.

Space is filled with wonders, but for years, man struggled to clearly see what was up there. Since May 20, 1990, the Hubble Space Telescope has provided images of galaxies and other celestial objects that, at one time, were only imagined. I'll admit these images are captivating, but all my life, the one thing I've wanted to see is what scientists call a fireball. As much as I've wanted to witness that heavenly fire show, I had never seen a blazing-across-the-night-sky, full-blown, burning-to-its-death, meteor. Well, you know what they say, "Just when you least expect it, IT happens."

On March 29, 2019, I was on my way to work as usual, driving through a dimly lit morning. Suddenly, at precisely 5:53 a.m. (yes, I looked), a very bright light, not far above the horizon, caught my eye. At first I thought it was a plane in distress, then it hit me! "That's a meteor!!" I shouted at my windshield. For the next five or six seconds, I watched that fireball of dying space rock as it streaked from the right to the left across the early morning sky. Then, almost as quickly as it had appeared, the show was over. "Man," I thought as the realization of what I had just witnessed sunk in, "all my life I've waited for that. And now, it's gone." I must have sounded like my grandchildren as I spoke aloud these words, "I want to do it again."

Once-in-a-lifetime. We all have those things that could happen but a single time in our lives. Some of us will never know what it is like to have our first child. Others will never know the thrill of winning the big game. I've seen more than sixty years of night skies and I've only witnessed one fireball. I realize that I could look outside tonight and see another, but, most likely, that was my once-in-a-lifetime moment. As unique as that experience was, I could have lived my entire life without seeing that fire in the sky, and I know that in the end, it doesn't matter. When all is said and done, the only thing that truly matters in our life on this earth is this: Did you receive God's gift of eternal salvation and His forgiveness of your sins?

Life is filled with memorable moments. The most important of these is not a heavenly fireball or, although very important, hearing the cry of our first-born child. The most important thing we will ever do is to make sure our sins have been forgiven by the One who created both us and that fireball. Seeing that fireball didn't complete my life; only God can do that. Don't wait a lifetime to do something you should have done a long time ago. Make this your once in a lifetime.

Father in Heaven. I thank You for the few seconds of child-like glee I experienced when I saw that flaming rock streak across the sky. But mostly, I thank You for the forgiveness of my sins and my promised heavenly home. Amen.

> *Therefore let no one judge you regarding food, or drink, or in respect of a holy day or new moon or sabbath days. These are shadows of things to come, but the substance belongs to Christ.*
> (Colossians 2:16-17)

THE MOON IS ALWAYS FULL

A full moon. When you look upward and see the moon shining in all its roundness, do you think, "Wow, what a beautiful sight"? Yes, sometimes the sight of a full moon can inspire awe, but years ago, when I was a paramedic, we always said a full moon inspired other things, especially if the moon was full on a Friday or a Saturday night. Those were the nights we knew we would get little, if any, sleep. It seems that a full moon is somehow bound to bring out the stupidity that usually lies dormant in some people.

People aren't the only things influenced by a full moon; ocean tides are affected by the white orb in the sky and animals take advantage of the lunar light to feed or to move about. But what about the times when the moon is only half-full, just a sliver in the night sky, or doesn't appear to be there at all? Did you ever wonder why we are told there's a New Moon up there when we look up and see no moon at all? You know, now that I think about it, isn't the moon always full?

The moon really doesn't shine; it simply reflects the light of the sun. The moon can't shine because it has no internal light source. When we look up at night into a cloudless sky and we don't see the moon, the moon is still there; it's just that the earth is between it and the sun. On those nights, what we see on the moon is not the sun's light but the earth's shadow.

It's like that with our Christian life. Just as the moon has no internal light source, we, too, do not have our own source of light. When we stand in the open and allow God's light, the source of our light, to fully strike us, the world can see God reflected by us. But when we allow the world to come between us and God, we can gradually lose our light. If we don't do what we can to avoid the world's influence, we will eventually find ourselves completely lost in the world's shadow. Just like we can't see the moon up there on a dark night, we are still here; we just can't be seen because the world is blocking us from God.

When we find ourselves becoming more and more hidden by the shadows of this world, we need to ask God to lead us from the shadow and into His light. Unlike the New Moon that cannot be seen, the us that is a new creation in Christ should be seen more than ever before. Just as the moon is best seen when it is "full," we must be a full Christian to best be seen by the world.

Father God. I pray others will see Your light as it reflects from me to the world. May You always guide me out of the shadows so I will always have a clear path to You. Amen.

But let the righteous be glad; let them rejoice before God; let them rejoice exceedingly. (Psalm 68:3)

AGAIN

"Do it again, Poppa!" "Again, Nana, again!" If you are a grandparent, you've no doubt heard those requests many times, or at least something along those lines. Grandkids, once they discover that you can do something that brings them pleasure or joy, will ask, actually it's closer to demand, again and again and again, that you do that special something, "Again!"

We all like the things we like. Some things we like more than others. And then there are those few things that we really, really like. Most of us have hobbies that, when we aren't doing it, we are thinking about the next time we will be able to do whatever it is. For me, that hobby would be fishing. You might notice that I didn't say catching fish – we can all dream. For a minute, let's talk food.

I don't know about you, but I like a relatively small number of dishes. Oh, I like steak (filet mignon) and I like some seafood but, if I were to go to a restaurant this very minute, I would go to my favorite Mexican place and I would order my favorite Mexican-inspired meal. What meal? A bed of rice with grilled chicken strips covered with queso dip and finally, that mound of food is topped with a heaping helping of fajita vegetables. If you ask me on Monday what I want to eat, there's your answer. If you ask me on Wednesday, guess what I'm going to say. And if you ask me again on Friday, yep, I could eat that same dish. After a while, when you hear my answer to the "what do I want to eat" question, you will probably say, "Again!? Really?"

I sometimes wonder if God thinks the same thing when some go to Him in prayer. "Again? After I've told you time and time that you can't handle being a millionaire? You're asking me again?" I know . . . if someone persistently asks for the wrong thing for the wrong reason, you know what they get? A persistent "No."

No, I don't ask God to make me a millionaire every time I talk to Him (I only did that once). Besides, I'm already working on my second million, I gave up on my first years ago.

Back to my grandkids. Sometimes, when they tell me to do it again, I have to tell them "No." I explain that Poppa doesn't have their energy. Man, if I could somehow bottle that stuff up, I wouldn't have to ask God for that millionaire thing. I still remember the night my granddaughter asked me if I wanted some of her energy. I told her thank you, but it's not quite that simple.

When I go to God, I must remember that my first priority should be just to thank Him for the blessings He has so abundantly given me. And if I truly want to experience the joy of being His child, I must remember the joy my grandchildren receive when I "do it again." I don't need to be a millionaire to be happy. I just need to remember the many times in my life that God has "done it again."

Heavenly Father. For the many gifts and blessings You have given me throughout my life, I thank You. And for all the blessings I have yet to experience, all I ask is You keep doing it again. Amen.

> *Therefore this I say and testify in the Lord, that from now on you walk not as other Gentiles walk, in the vanity of their minds, having their understanding darkened, excluded from the life of God through the ignorance that is within them, due to the hardness of their hearts.* (Ephesians 4:17-18)

THE LOST CIRCLE WALK

I've never been lost, at least in the physical sense (we've all been spiritually lost). I'm talking about the kind of lost where you find yourself having no idea of where you are and you don't have the slightest inkling of how you are going to become "not lost." You know, the kind of lost that happens in the movies or certain National Parks, a Louisiana bayou, or maybe a jungle; the kind of lost that makes you say, "This can't be good."

As a long-time movie watcher, there are some movies that I have seen more than once. They are well written, having a plot that makes you want to see what happens more than once. One of those movies that I've seen multiple times is the 1997 film, *The Edge*. Without divulging too much, sometime into the movie, a small plane crashes and three men find themselves lost deep in the Alaskan wilderness. They take stock of their predicament and quickly determine that they will have to walk out.

Their plan must be foolproof because I've heard the same plan many times. Walk until you find a river, follow the river until you find a road, follow the road until you find a house, a town, or a kind stranger, and it's at that point your condition changes from lost to found. The only problem with this plan is it seems to always end the same way; the walk begins, lasts for a few hours, and ends at the very place you started. You've just performed your version of the Lost Circle Walk. Because most of us aren't very good at unaided navigation, we tend to walk in circles when lost. And yes, the men in the movie had their version of the same circular walk.

When someone is lost without a compass, a map, or a trusted guide, that someone usually wanders until they are found, some wild animal kills them, or they die, alone, in the wilderness. When we are lost in our sin and we try to find our own way out of that problem, we usually end up going around in circles. We always wind up right back where we started, just as lost and having no idea of how to become un-lost. We continue down the same path; we sin and sin some more, never knowing just how close we were to taking the right path, the one that leads to our salvation, all the while, wasting more and more time trying to save ourselves.

Just as the lost person in the wilderness needs a guide, the person lost in sin needs a guide to save them. The men in the movie finally found that river and a canoe that they used to find a lake. Only after building a fire to create the smoke that was seen by a helicopter were they finally rescued. Only when we send out a call for Jesus to help us can we be saved from our sinful life.

Want to be saved? You'll need Jesus to guide you out. Or, you could just continue walking around and around in circles. By the way, how's that working out?

> *Lord Jesus. I thank You for guiding me from my life that was lost in sin to the salvation that is Your eternal cleansing. I pray others would stop their walking in circles and call to You for the help they need. Amen.*

> *Caleb silenced the people before Moses and said, "Let us go up at once and possess it, for we are able to overcome it."*
> (Numbers 13:30)

WHY NOT?

Look on the bright side. Who am I kidding? It's so much easier to be negative. It seems our modern world looks at everything with the intention of finding the bad – or at least the not so good. Tom, a fellow we all know, is running a tad late for work. He's stuck at a busy intersection trying to merge into traffic. His blinker is doing its thing as Tom stares at other drivers as they close gaps, refusing to let him in. Tom counts as ten cars, then fifteen, drive slowly by, none of the drivers willing to let Tom in the slowly advancing line. Tom curses himself for being late nearly as much as he curses the other drivers who could, if they chose, let him ease into the traffic. Finally, a driver slows, and waves Tom in. Tom waves back, thanking the young driver. But on the inside, Tom is fuming and having to resist the temptation to ram the car in front of him for being so inconsiderate.

We go to a fine restaurant and, after a ten-minute wait for a table, we sit down to what we know will be a good meal. Even though the food was very good, we have grown irritated because our server was slower than we consider acceptable. Never mind the fact that you are her first solo table because her trainer had to leave to take her child to the doctor. You nod politely at her apology, but you have made up your mind that her "excuses" won't persuade you to leave your normal tip.

We can think of ten "Debbie Downers" but we struggle to name two "Enthusiastic Eddies." Mark 11:24 tells us that when we pray, we are to make our request as if it – whatever "it" is – had already occurred. Too often, however, our prayers are not spoken with the confidence of faith but with seeds of doubt. Instead of focusing on the good things God has in store for us, we find it easier to remember our rough times and disappointments. We concentrate on the giants that await us in the form of problems or the potholes in the highway of our life. We focus on the uphill struggle to the top of the mountain never thinking about the downhill stroll that awaits us on the other side.

In the 13th and 14th chapters of Numbers, we discover that God instructed Moses to send twelve spies into the land of Canaan to gather information and to return with a report of the things they found. Although the land held great promise, it was a focus on the negative by ten of the twelve that resulted in the Israelites having to wander through the desert for forty additional years. Yes, those ten agreed with Caleb and Joshua that the land was rich and held great promise, but they just couldn't get past the fact that the people of the land were giants that seemed impossible to defeat. When facing our problems, we can see the "impossible to cross" Red Sea or we can see the path that God can provide by parting the waters.

Instead of remaining focused on why we can't, should we not embrace the possibility of the why not?

Dear Jesus. Let me remember that You faced Your problems with a faith that God would be there with You, no matter how difficult the situation. When I am challenged with life's difficulties, let me remember that I can either see the water or the path. Amen.

And a woman having a hemorrhage for twelve years, who had spent all her living on physicians, but could not be healed by anyone, came behind Him, and touched the fringe of His garment. And immediately her hemorrhage dried up. Jesus said, "Who touched Me?" When everyone denied it, Peter and those who were with Him said, "Master, the crowds are pressing against You, and You say, 'Who touched Me?'" But Jesus said, "Someone touched Me, for I perceive that power has gone out from Me." (Luke 8:43-46)

THE TRANSFER

From time-to-time, my job requires me to do some research, typically about things associated with how one can safely work around electricity. While reading about the conductive ability of different metals and alloys, I discovered this: Heat always flows (transfers) from the hotter object to the cooler object. The cooler object will always absorb heat; the hotter object never absorbs cool. After a while, if unable to replenish its heat, the object that began as the hottest will lose enough of its heat that both objects, if they are capable of doing so, will equalize and will be the same temperature.

So it is between us and Jesus. As we grow closer and closer to Jesus, we begin to absorb righteousness from Him. No matter how close we get to Him, He will never absorb our unrighteousness. We will never make Jesus less holy; we are the ones who will always become more holy because of our interaction with Him. Unlike that hot object having to be re-heated because its heat is absorbed by the cool object, the reservoir of Jesus' righteousness will never need to be replenished, no matter how much of His righteousness is transferred into us.

The story from Luke, chapter eight, gives meaning to this example. For twelve years, a woman had been continuously sick. No amount of money spent and no earthly physician had been able to relieve her ailment. I imagine she had nearly reached the point of giving in and accepting her lot in life.

We don't know who told her, but somehow she heard that Jesus was a man who was able to heal the sick. I can see her praying that somehow Jesus would find His way into her village. And when she heard that Jesus would be passing through her village, she made up her mind that she was going see this man, no matter the cost or the struggle. When the day of His visit finally arrived, she, after being blocked time and again by the crowd, dropped to her hands and knees and crawled through the crowd until she touched, not Jesus, but the edge of the hem of His garment.

This woman never touched Jesus, but, because of her faith and her dogged persistence, she was able to get close enough to Him that His healing power was transferred to her. We know this because Jesus told us that He felt it when the power left Him. Her sickness did not go to Jesus; His healing power went to her.

My little Chihuahua, Gracie, can't wait for me to light the gas logs on a cold winter's evening. She just loves lying in front of the fire and soaking up its heat. Gracie absorbs the fire's heat; the fire doesn't absorb her cold. We will never be more like Jesus by expelling our unrighteousness toward Him. The only way we will ever become more like Jesus is to get close enough so that we can soak Him up.

Jesus my Savior. Thank You for the story about the sick woman and how she was able to get close enough to You so Your healing power could enter her. I pray I will have the faith of that sick woman so that I will always seek You first and I will always want more and more of You. Amen.

And "the sow that was washed to her wallowing in the mud."
(2 Peter 2:22b)

ONLY ONE MUDHOLE

Over the years, I've had a few pets. Most of them – including the two I have now – have been dogs. I have always been pretty much a dog person. Other than dogs, I've owned, at different times and for different reasons, the following animals: a single cat (it's a long story), two ferrets (instinct on four feet), and fish, both fresh and salt water. Now that I think of it, fish aren't really pets but they are animals and I have owned and fed them, so they qualify. Seeing it from that point of view, I haven't really had much of a variety when it comes to pet ownership. I've known people who've had birds, snakes (why?), lizards (again, why?), spiders (seriously?), even a Capuchin monkey. All of these are great, but . . . pigs?

I read stories of people who own a pet pig. They swear pigs are the perfect pet. (I was also told that lie about a ferret, hmmm). After all, pigs are supposed to be fairly smart. But a pig? When I think of a pig, it usually includes images of ham or pork chops or everyone's favorite, bacon. The more I think about it, I'm not sure about having a pet pack of bacon. When I buy bacon, it's not a pet kind of relationship I'm looking for. Anyway, I'm told that those who have pet pigs keep them clean and can often be found walking their little piggy through the neighborhood. If I know anything about a pig (other than being tasty), it's this: pigs like mud.

Imagine this, your pet pig has a favorite mudhole. Each time that pig gets muddy, you give it a bath. No matter how many times you bathe that pig, if you give that pig half a chance, I'll wager that it will gladly go straight back to that mudhole. You have to remember, the cleanest pig in the world is only one good mudhole away from looking like every other pig. I can't imagine a pig preferring a living room carpet over a good mudhole.

If you think about it, we can be like that pig. We can take 1,000 baths using the finest French-milled lavender soap. We can put on cologne or perfume that costs $1,000 an ounce. We can dress up in tailor-made suits and carry alligator handbags. We can change our outward appearance so much that the world will swear we are living a changed life. But, without an inward change, we will soon find ourselves yearning for the good old days and our favorite mudhole.

Romans 12:2 warns us not to be conformed by the world. The book of Second Corinthians 5:17 tells us that one who is in Christ is a new creation. Finally, we find these words just a few verses earlier: "For this reason we do not lose heart: Even though our outward man is perishing, yet our inward man is being renewed day by day" (2 Corinthians 4:16).

Anyone can fool the world by being a clean-cut, well-dressed church attender. But if that is all that person is, someday soon they will be found in their old clothes wallowing in their favorite mudhole. Christians may be a lot of things but there are two things a real Christian is not. Real Christians aren't pigs, and real Christians don't like spiritual mud.

Dear Jesus. Thank You for cleansing my innermost being. I know that cleansing took me out of the mudhole of my old life and made me acceptable for the heavenly life that is to come. Amen.

> *My heart and my body cry out for the living God.*
> *(Psalm 84:2b)*

CRAVING OXYGEN

The dictionary defines a craving as an intense, urgent, or abnormal desire or longing. Some of us have experienced a craving for a particular treat and nothing else can satisfy that craving. But think about this: Have you ever craved something that is much more life sustaining than a simple treat?

According to the Guinness Book of World Records, on February 28, 2016, in Barcelona, Spain, Aleix Segura Vendrel, held his breath for an astounding twenty-four minutes and three seconds! And he did this voluntarily. You're telling me Mr. Vendrel didn't have anything better to do than to jump into a pool and hold his breath for more than a third of an hour? I can remember a time I sat on the bottom of a pool (I was in waist-deep water) and held my breath for a little longer than a minute. I couldn't wait to break the surface so I could draw my next breath of life-sustaining oxygen. I can only imagine how Mr. Vendrel's lungs felt after more than twenty-four minutes. Scratch that, I can't imagine that; I don't even want to try.

The Bible tells us we are to crave God's presence in our life. Every cell in our body and every fiber of our being was created to serve God. When we feel ourselves being pulled away from God by our sin and disobedience, we need to stand to our feet and rise above those things that take our attention from God. We must rise above the fog of our sinful life, expel our stale, sinful desires, and inhale deeply the breath of forgiveness that only God can provide. God is what we crave, and only God will satisfy the longing we have for that fulfilled life that we so desperately want.

Navy Seals must be able to hold their breath long enough to swim fifty meters under water. Some species of whale can hold their breath for nearly two hours. Marine iguanas have been known to hold their breath for eighty minutes as they search for food. And since we are naming different species, the emperor penguin will hold its breath for twenty minutes as it dives and hunts for fish. All of these, and many more species, have proven that they can hold their breath. Eventually, no matter how long they do, each will reach a point that they must breach the surface and take a deep breath of oxygen.

If you ever see a video of a whale breaching the surface, notice one thing. When that whale finally breaks through that surface, the first thing it does is to blow out the old so that it can take in the new. To receive new life, we must first empty ourselves of our stale, sinful life in order to fully take in the new life that is only given by Christ. Of all the things we can crave, God is the one craving that absolutely nothing else will satisfy.

Eternal Savior. Thank You for meeting my every need. When I find myself sinking into the depths, I pray that You will reach down and pull me upward to the breath that comes from You, the breath that always renews my strength. Amen.

> *See, this only have I found: that God made man upright, but they have sought out many schemes.* (Ecclesiastes 7:29)

A Work In Progress

Over the years, I have discovered that writing is filled with many "do-overs." I'll sit down, either in front of my computer or at a table with a pen and paper (the way the scribes of old did it) and begin typing or writing a story. My job requires me to type reports or to develop computer-based training programs. Whenever I begin a report, I always add a watermark across the page. In big, capital letters, the word "DRAFT" will show itself to anyone who needs to see the report. Only after the report has received the necessary approvals and is ready for publication will I remove the watermark from the pages. The report is no longer a draft; it is a finished product.

As I grow older, I realize that, while life is filled with drafts, there is one thing God has taught me: While we may not be complete, we are not a draft. When God created man, He didn't take a lump of clay, shape it, look at it, and say, "Nope. The nose ain't right." When I read from the first book of the Bible, I learn, "Then the Lord God formed man from the dust of the ground and breathed into his nostrils the breath of life, and man became a living being" (Genesis 2:7). Additionally, according to Genesis 1:26, God formed us in "our image." We were formed in the image of God, Jesus, and the Holy Spirit.

One of the first things God did to improve Adam's lot in life is found in Genesis 2:22 when He formed the first woman from one of Adam's ribs so he – Adam – could have a helper and a companion. Later, after the imperfection of sin entered the story, God didn't sit down and start over. He didn't highlight us and hit the delete key. Even when He destroyed the world with the great flood, He didn't wipe out the entire human race.

I've looked all over me and I can't find a watermark anywhere. I am not a draft. Despite my imperfections, I am still created in the image of God, Jesus, and the Holy Spirit. I may not be – no, I am definitely not – perfect. However, despite those imperfections, I am perfect for the work that God would have me do.

Whatever it is that He asks us to do, let us not limit God. Let us be reminded that we are not a draft. We should remember that we always have been, and we are now, a work in progress.

Father God. I thank You that, whatever it is You have in store for me, You are still working on me. And I know that one day I will be the perfect creation You intended. Amen.

> *Yet the hour is coming, and is now here, when the true worshippers will worship the Father in spirit and truth. For the Father seeks such to worship Him. God is Spirit, and those who worship Him must worship Him in spirit and truth.*
> (John 4:23-24)

THE "PERFECT" WORSHIP SERVICE

Over the years, I have been to various types of worship services. I've been to those that seemingly lasted forever and I've been to others that ended well before I wanted. Some I liked more than others, but I can honestly say that in most of those worship services, I left the sanctuary knowing more about God than I did when I entered. I also learned some other things. You want an example? Okay, let's talk church music.

As I've aged, I realize that I miss some of the older stuff. Sometimes, the music is a bit loud, other times, I would be okay if the music were a touch – not much – but a touch louder. I like a lot of the traditional hymns, but I also like a lot of the modern worship songs, some of them so much that I've downloaded them to enjoy again and again. While I like some of the modern updates to the traditional hymns, honestly, some of them, in my opinion, were better left alone. Having said that, I realize not everyone likes the same styles of music. Face it, music ministers have a tough job.

How about the environment of the sanctuary? Why is the lighting either too bright or nearly too dim to see? Is it too hard to get the temperature right? I've been in some church buildings that are too hot and others that made me think, "Are they trying to hang meat in here?" I've heard these comments about the youth: "That's a lively young crowd," or "Don't they know they're in church?" I like the media screens, but I know some who wish they could hold a hymnal just one more time. And let's not forget the length of the sermon. It's either perfect or, "Does he know how long the line is once the Methodists get there?"

In truth, if our focus is on the songs that were sung, or not, the temperature of the building, the hardness of the pew cushions, the smile of the usher, or our overall level of personal comfort, we will most likely miss the perfect part of the worship service. Yes, creature comforts are needed. It's hard to focus if you are dripping sweat on your Bible because the sanctuary is 100 degrees or your feet are turning blue because they are cold. But if our physical comfort is our primary focus, is there a chance we might miss the spiritual comfort that God wants to give us?

Let's face it, no building is ever perfect, even a church building. No one will ever like every song and some would have complained if they had attended the Sermon on the Mount because it was held in an outdoor arena. When we stop seeking the perfect worship service and begin seeking the perfect reason for our worship, only then will we begin to experience "perfect" worship.

Lord Jesus. Thank You for the church I attend. Thank You for the men of God You have placed in that pulpit. I pray I will silence my complaints so that I will be able to hear from You in every service. Amen.

And be renewed in the spirit of your mind; and that you put on the new nature, which was created according to God in righteousness and true holiness. (Ephesians 4:23-24)

OUT WITH THE OLD

I like a good cobbler. No, I'm not talking about someone who repairs shoes, although when I need shoe repairs, I want a cobbler who is good at what they do. I'm talking about the cobbler that comes from the oven. Either with a scoop of vanilla ice cream or not (I realize that, to some, warm cobbler without ice cream is food blasphemy), I like cobbler. Not wanting to brag, but I've been told that I make a pretty decent cobbler. I make peach, peach/mango, fresh pineapple, fresh blueberry, fresh blackberry, fresh cherry, and fresh apple (I seem to have developed a "fresh" pattern). Some of you may be wondering, "Why not pear?" Simple, I'm not a pear fan. Sorry. Back to my story, in the world of dessert, it's just hard to beat a good, made-from-scratch, cobbler.

Sometimes, I'll begin to make one and the smell of the flour will catch my attention. For lack of a better description, the flour will smell "old." When I smell that "old flour" smell, I dump it in the trash and open a fresh bag. I've been told you can't tell when flour is old, but I know it's old so it's out with the old and in with the new.

When we become Christians, we – through the guidance of the Holy Spirit – must look at our lives and get rid of those things that can give our life an "old' taste or feel. Some things are easy to identify. Do you have a habit of using profanity? Get rid of it. How about gossip? Stop it. Are you a complainer, overly critical, prideful, do you judge, or is your decision about someone based on skin color or gender? If you do any of those things (and most of us are guilty), they can prevent someone from entering into a full, brand new relationship with God. How do you get rid of them? Ask God for His help.

You may have had these habits so long that you don't recognize them as sinful. Pray that God will reveal those things in your life (you can't throw it out if you don't know it's there) and that He will help you rid yourself of these old habits.

If your closet is like mine, you have clothes that you haven't worn for years. Your pantry probably has canned goods that need tossing. Look toward the back or the bottom of your freezer and you'll most likely find food that is long past its "best if used by" date. I can throw those out. And when I throw out the old life, I must make sure I never go through that garbage again.

Eternal Father. Thank You for cleaning up my life. I pray that You will cast Your light on anything that may be hiding in some forgotten corner of my life that would cause me to stumble backward to my old ways so I can rid it from my life. Amen.

> *Therefore, if any man is in Christ, he is a new creature. Old things have passed away. Look, all things have become new.*
> (2 Corinthians 5:17)

CHANGE IS A TWO-WAY REQUEST

Give and take. You scratch my back and I'll scratch yours. What's in it for me? It seems that life is filled with giving something and receiving something in return. Some consider that to be the way business is done. If I ask you to do something for me, I should expect sometime in the future you would come to me asking for a return of the favor. If someone is moving, in order to save a little money, they often attempt to borrow someone with a truck to help them move. If you are that someone that made the request, you may hope you never have to return the favor but you will, if you are ever asked.

But not everyone who receives a favor is in the mood to reciprocate when called upon. There are those out there who not only hope they won't be asked to return the favor; they don't even take the call when it comes. It doesn't take too long for those people to develop the reputation of being, "all take and no give." In the neighborhood of favors, they live on the one-way street where all favors come to them, and no favors leave for others.

Think about salvation for a moment. Someone realizes they are a sinner. They try to clean up their own sin but they eventually discover that their efforts are in vain. They finally turn to Jesus, the only one who can cleanse sin from someone's life and ask for forgiveness. If they are sincere in that request and they do so in faith, the Bible tells us they are saved. ". . . that if you confess with your mouth Jesus is Lord, and believe in your heart that God has raised Him from the dead, you will be saved" (Romans 10:9). That's the way salvation works.

When it comes to salvation, some people want all the benefits and none of the alleged limitations. They want Jesus to clean the sin from their life, but they really don't want to change the way they live. It's as if they think salvation is a hall pass that allows someone to continue living a sinful and carefree life without any consequence. While that sounds great, there's a problem with that line of thinking; it's not Biblical. Hebrews 10:26, First John 3:6, and First John 3:8 are three of many verses that tell us we can't be saved and continue living a sinful life.

Someone that continues to willfully sin after asking for salvation is kind of like playing in the mud, changing clothes, and getting right back in the same mud. If they insist on getting back in the mud, they'll never know how it is to be clean. Besides, when someone is sincere in their request, they are going to change how they live because God's Holy Spirit has taken up residence in their heart.

Salvation is a two-way partnership. Jesus does the cleaning and we, in accordance with His will, do the living. If you're thinking otherwise, think again.

Eternal Savior. I pray that I would never take for granted the sacrifice You made for the forgiveness of my sins. I pray that my outward life will reflect my inward change. Amen.

> *As everyone has received a gift, even so serve one another with it, as good stewards of the manifold grace of God.*
> (1 Peter 4:10)

THE GRACIOUS SERVANT

"Good morning. It's good to see you. How are you doing on this fine morning? What may I get for you?" For some of us, that may be a little syrupy or cheesy. Okay, would you rather I say, "What do you want?" Is that better? At its heart, each of these questions, although very different, are asking the same thing: "How may I serve you?"

We may be tempted to think good service is hard to find. And if we focus on our negative experiences, good service seems to be in rare form these days. We can all name example after example of those times when we stood in one of the big box stores and wanted to scream aloud, "Does anyone work here?!?" As much as this may sound familiar, I disagree that good service has completely disappeared from daily life.

Recently, I was sitting in a Cracker Barrel restaurant enjoying my typical Sunrise Sampler. My food was just as ordered, the orange juice was cold, and my coffee was hot. It was early and, as I am apt to do, I was people watching. As she darted from table to table, I noticed my server and the way she carried herself. On her way back to the kitchen area, she stopped at my table and asked me if everything was all right.

While watching her with the other diners, her compassionate demeanor had been obvious. Now, as she stood next to my table, I asked her if I could ask her a question (actually, that was a question, but go with me here). She nodded her head and said yes.

"Are you a Christian?"

"Yes, sir. I am."

"It shows."

During the following two minutes, I learned that she opened every day with a prayer that, through her job, others would see and hear Christ in the way she carried herself and the words she spoke. I thanked her and, when I paid my bill, I left her a note with a generous tip. My note? "He knows and He shows."

We are quick to remember bad service and bad servants. Why is it that some of us are so quick to fire off a bad comment on social media when we receive bad service, but we won't take the same time to compliment a restaurant or some other business when the service we receive is good? We never think that the person who is serving us may have been told that tonight was their last night on the job because the restaurant is closing, or they had to leave a sick child with a sitter because the money from this job is all the family has to live on.

The next time we have an opportunity to serve others, remember these words of the Bible: "Whoever says he remains in Him ought to walk as He walked" (1 John 2:6) and the words of Paul when he said, "Follow me as I follow Christ" (1 Corinthians 11:1). If we aren't finding opportunities to serve, perhaps we should remember the advice from the opening verse, "Use it [the gift you received from God] to serve others."

Believe me, if our focus is on finding bad things, bad things will be found. But we need to remember that someone you meet during the day could have asked God to show them that good still exists. You may be the good they need to see. Yes, we may have had a bad experience but we might be the Jesus experience someone needs to have.

My Savior. I pray You will allow me to be the good someone needs to see as I walk through the life You have given me. Let others see and hear You through me. Amen.

> *While we do not look at the things which are seen, but at the things which are not seen. For the things which are seen are temporal, but the things which are not seen are eternal.*
> (2 Corinthians 4:18)

FOOTPRINTS ON THE MOON

September 12, 1962. President John Fitzgerald Kennedy stood before thousands of people in Houston, Texas. As many presidents had before him and every president has since, President Kennedy had many opportunities to address our nation. But on this day in Rice Stadium, President Kennedy made a bold statement; to some, what he proclaimed was downright preposterous. The president declared that we, the United States of America, would send a man to the moon.

For a minute, imagine that you are in 1962 America. For most households, color television was only a dream. Telephones were wired to a wall. For the most part, computers were huge and bulky; the cell phone we take for granted has thousands of times more computing power than anything that existed in 1962. And yet, here was the president telling his country that we were going to send a man to the moon. "We choose to go to the moon. We choose to go to the moon this decade." In a time when buses or trains were the prominent methods of long-distance travel, President Kennedy was telling us that we would send someone TO THE MOON!

President Kennedy stood on that stage and made that statement not because it had been done before; he made that statement because he believed it could be done. Fast forward to July 20, 1969. More than five years after his untimely death, the words of that president rang true when Neil Armstrong's foot stepped from a ladder and made the first human footprint on the surface of the moon. "That's one small step for man, one giant leap for mankind," Armstrong declared.

Today, more than fifty years after that historic mission to our nearest celestial neighbor, there are those who refuse to believe any of it actually took place. Much the same as the moon landing skeptics, there are those, despite evidence to the contrary, who refuse to believe that Jesus died on a cross and, after being in a tomb for more than two days, rose from that tomb. Even Thomas, one of Jesus' closest followers, said he could not believe until his eyes told him it was true. "But he said to them, 'Unless I see the nail prints in His hands, and put my finger in the nail prints, and put my hand in His side, I will not believe'" (John 20:25b). Only a week later, Jesus appeared again, this time with Thomas present, "Then He said to Thomas, 'Put your finger here, and look at My hands. Put your hand here and place it in My side. Do not be faithless, but believing'" (John 20:27).

Do I believe Neil Armstrong walked on the moon? I sure do. Do I believe Jesus died on a cross for my sins? Yes. And do I believe He arose from the tomb, alive and no longer dead? So much so that I have bet my eternal soul on it. I didn't need to be on the moon to believe, and I didn't need to be outside the garden tomb to believe. As much as I believe there are human footprints on the moon, I believe Jesus left footprints as He walked from the tomb.

Lord Jesus. When I struggle with doubt, remind me, yes, You did walk from the tomb. Tell me just as You told Thomas; if you must touch Me to believe, touch Me. Just believe. Amen.

> *Seek the Lord and His strength; seek His face continually.*
> (1 Chronicles 16:11)

BEING IN SYNC

Being out of sync. Askew. Out of whack. Catawhompus. Half-a-bubble off. No matter how you say it, we like things to be . . . in order. Have you ever watched a television program and found yourself becoming annoyed because the words you heard were not synced up to the movement of the speaker's mouth? I'm not talking about the old Godzilla movies that were filmed in Japan and introduced to the American audience with English-speaking voice-overs. I'm talking about a program where there is a noticeable difference between hearing the voice and seeing the mouth move. I don't know about you, but this drives me nuts. I usually find myself thinking, "Surely I'm not the only one who sees this."

Synchronized. Not the easiest word to spell and for some, not the easiest word to say. In our modern world of having to abbreviate practically everything, you are most likely to hear this word in its abbreviated form: sync. When a car's transmission doesn't sync up with the engine, it is said they don't mesh. Believe me, when a car's transmission and engine don't mesh, the car don't go, emphasis on don't.

In order for a Christian to be the best Christian possible, it is imperative that they are synchronized with God. Being out of sync with God means we are either ahead of, or behind, wherever it is that God wants us to be. And the more out of sync with God we are, the more out of sorts our lives become. Why, you may wonder, is the divorce rate in our country nearing 50% of all marriages? Because we aren't in sync with God's wishes for us. We see the person WE want and we never ask God what He thinks. Why do so many young people choose to end their life when they have a whole lifetime ahead of them? Because God's plan and their plan don't sync. Old Testament Job went through a rough time. He lost his children and his fortune. His friends seemed to be against him, and his wife was telling him to just give up. Job could have easily gotten out of sync with God, but in the final chapter of his book, after God had asked Job a number of questions, we hear Job's answer, "I know that You can do everything, and that no thought can be withheld from You" (Job 42:2). While most of us would have fallen out of sync with God, Job didn't.

If we are out of sync with God, with whom are we in sync? Could it be possible that we are in sync with the anti-god? Satan tells us that God is too big and that – to God – our problems are just like us, insignificant in the big picture. Our fears, our hopelessness, and most of our problems come not from God but from our failure to synchronize our lives with His wishes for us. Second Timothy 1:7 tells us that God gave us a spirit of love, power, and self-control, not fear.

When we find ourselves floundering through life, we need to stop what we're doing and turn away from where we're going. We need to sit down, shut up, and sync our lives with the One who gave that life to us.

Heavenly Father. I pray You will always correct me when I sync my life to me instead of to You. Amen.

> *I, even I, am He who blots out your transgressions for My own sake, and will not remember your sins.* (Isaiah 43:25)

THE SPECIALIST

How can something so little cause so much pain? How little? Kidney stone little. How many of us have suffered through a kidney stone? As of this writing, in my sixtieth year, I have been humbled by the attacks (a more than apt description) of those little deposits since I was twenty-three. Last year, one visited me during the Independence Day holiday and this year, one made for a very laborious Labor Day. It's hard to believe that something so small can have such a large influence on one's well being.

I have a dentist with whom I'm on a first name basis. I trust him with pretty much anything having to do with my teeth. If I were to have an issue on his off day, I can call his cell phone and he will do what he can to make my day better. As good as he is with my teeth, I never once thought about calling him about my kidney stones. Why not? He's a doctor, and a good one, but he's a dentist, not a urologist. Likewise, if I'm discussing an upcoming lithotripsy procedure with my urologist, I'm not going to ask him why my vehicle's transmission is slipping.

Life, it seems, is full of problems. Some problems are general and can be handled by pretty much anyone. What do you do when can't see because your light bulb has blown? Simple, you replace it. If you stop at a gas pump because you're low on fuel, do you need a specialist to "fill 'er up"? No. You handle it. But some problems do require a specialist. Like brain surgery or a heart transplant. If I have either of those, I want the best doctor available. And then, there's sin.

Sin is the one problem we all have. Not everyone will have cancer, and not everyone will need a heart transplant, but, according to Romans 3:23, everyone has the sin problem. And everyone's sins, while similar, are different and they are personal. Being sin sick, like some other ailments, most likely won't be noticed by others. While there are many doctors who can treat cancer, there is only one doctor who can treat sin. Only God defined what sin is, so only God can forgive sin.

When the time comes for me to replace the roof on my house, I'll call a roofer. If I find myself in legal trouble, I'll call a lawyer. If my Mercury Optimax gives me trouble, I'm calling Clint because he's the best boat motor mechanic I know. But for sin removal, I don't call just any specialist. I'm calling *The* Specialist. When it comes to my sin problem, only God will do.

Lord God. I am sorry I have disappointed You so many times. I know without You and Your forgiveness, I would be destined for an eternity separated from You and Your goodness. Thank You for forgiving me of my sins. Amen.

> *Then Philip spoke, beginning with the same Scripture, and preached Jesus to him.* (Acts 8:35)

PASS IT ON

How many of you know a secret way to do something? It may be an old family recipe to cook chicken and dumplings or chili. It may be that mechanic who knows the little tricks it takes to properly change a set of brake pads. How about using that "secret" side street (at least it used to be a secret) when you are going to the football game. I'm sure there are those in our government who are working on some "Top Secret" project that I hope keeps our country safe.

Because I have been using certain computer applications for many years, I long ago saw the benefit of learning and using keyboard shortcuts as I type. It didn't take long to discover that using a keyboard shortcut was much quicker than moving the mouse, selecting some text or a spreadsheet cell, clicking an icon, then selecting an option from a dropdown list. Many times, my boss has told me he wants to learn all of my tricks. I've told him I'll be glad to show him but my "tricks" aren't a secret; they are available to anyone. When it comes to helping someone be more productive or saving time and aggravation, I'm happy to help.

We, as Christians, are told to do the same thing. We have been given the knowledge of a path that guarantees a better future for any who want it. That knowledge, like pretty much a majority of knowledge, is no secret. There is no combination of computer keys that have to be pressed in a certain order or secret ingredient that gives a meal a certain "umph" or a special road that only we and 10,000 other people know about.

For nearly 2,000 years, this knowledge has been available in the form of a free gift for all who care to receive it. Our job, as those who have received that gift, is to tell others how they can receive the same gift. We can talk about the gift or write about it, but regardless of our communication method, our job is to share what the gift has done for us and what it can do for others.

We may go to our grave with that recipe, but, when it comes to the saving knowledge that is salvation through Christ, we must not let others go to their grave without passing it on.

Lord Jesus. I pray You will give me the words to say to those who need to hear about Your free gift of eternal salvation.
Amen.

> *And be kind one to another, tenderhearted, forgiving one another, just as God in Christ also forgave you.*
> (Ephesians 4:32)

THE END OF THE ROPE

Rope is a tool that is so common at many workplaces that it seldom stands out. It is used to secure things, connect things, pull things, or to hoist things. Look in any mountain climber's tool kit and you will probably find more than one coil of multi-colored rope. Rope can be used to save life or to end life. It can be found in countless color combinations and made from many different materials. Rope is one of those everyday things that comes with its own saying.

To be at the end of one's rope is typically said when someone finds themselves in a bad spot. When we have reached the limit of our patience with someone or something, we find ourselves at the end of our proverbial rope. Sometimes, during times of high stress, our rope may seem shorter than normal. When that rope is associated with a relationship, it's what we do when we are nearing the end of that particular piece of rope.

Some of those relationships simply end. That "one more last time" was truly the last time. For other relationships, you will determine that it is worth salvaging. You love or care about that person with whom your rope is at its end enough to give them at least one more try. You forgive the transgression and you start over.

Can you imagine how many times God has been near the end of His rope with us? Or more accurately, if you were God, how many times would you be willing to forgive you of the same sin? In the book of Matthew, Jesus was asked by Peter if he must forgive someone as many as seven times when they sin against someone. "Jesus said to him, 'I do not say to you up to seven times, but up to seventy times seven'" (Matthew 18:22). Jesus didn't mean we are to forgive someone 490 times before we reach the end of our forgiveness; Jesus meant that we are to forgive someone as many times as they ask forgiveness.

How are we to forgive? According to the opening verse, we are to forgive others just as God forgave us. While it is easy to forgive most people, there are some people that, because of continued offenses, we may not want to forgive. It is then we must remember that, according to Romans 3:23, we are all sinners. In First John 1:9, we read that God is faithful to forgive our sins. If He forgives us, we must find it in our heart to forgive others.

Yes, forgiving others is sometimes hard. It's during the times we are tempted to cut our rope with others that we must remember that God's rope with us has no end.

Father God. I thank You that You have forgiven me of all my sins. I pray You will grant me the same spirit of forgiveness to others. And I pray my rope with You never reaches its end.
Amen.

> *"All things are lawful to me," but not all things are helpful. "All things are lawful for me," but I will not be brought under the power of anything.* (1 Corinthians 6:12)

MODERATION

As I grow older, I hear that I must practice moderation when it comes to some things in my life. I'm told that I should eat more fruits and vegetables and less of other things. The problem with eating more plants is a little thing known as an oxalate. Plant-based oxalates can be found in a lot of plants and most of those plants are supposed to be good for me.

I'll admit it; I like potatoes. Potatoes happen to be one of my favorite plants to eat. They are one of my dietary staples. If I could get away with it, I would eat potatoes, in one form or another, pretty much every day. If a potato could be my friend, me and old spud would be what you call, "Besties." However, oxalates also like potatoes. So much so that I've pretty much cut potatoes out of my diet.

What's so bad about oxalates? Oxalates are one of the primary chemicals that form kidney stones, at least the type of kidney stones I have. And as much as I like potatoes, I dislike kidney stones even more. And since I am attempting to moderate my kidney stone episodes, I have had to exercise a great deal of moderation when it comes to potatoes.

Moderation. Most of us would be a lot better off if we simply moderated the things we do or consume. Over the past couple of years, I have really cut back on the time I spend watching television and I can't say that I'm worse off for it. Television was relatively easy. Red meat, fried foods, pork, sweetened tea, and, yes, potatoes are much harder to moderate than watching my 50" plasma television.

All of that moderation stuff is great, but there are things a majority of us need to do more. Communicate with others, sleep (with moderation), exercise, be honest, be kind, eat low-fat foods, eat more vegetables, are just a few of the things that can enrich our daily lives and probably make us all a bit more healthy. How about God?

Of all the things we have, daily Bible study and prayer are two things we emphasize if we want to have a deep relationship with God. The only way we will ever grow our relationship with God and His Son, Jesus, is to spend more of our time with each of them.

Yes, because of oxalates, I've had to change a lot of my eating habits. I consume more milk and fewer potatoes. And because years ago I made a conscious decision to de-moderate my time with God, I've spent more time reading about, and talking to, Him. With some things in life, moderation is fine. But when it comes to God and Jesus, you truly cannot get enough.

Heavenly Father. Thank You for the many gifts You have given us that enrich our lives. I pray You will grant me the willpower to consume with moderation those things that have proven to cause me harm. And I pray I will exercise less moderation when it comes to spending time with You. Amen.

For now we see as through a glass, dimly, but then, face to face. Now I know in part, but then I shall know, even as I also am known. (1 Corinthians 13:12)

CLOSER THAN APPEARANCES

If there is one thing life is guaranteed to bring, it's change. I was born in 1959. I recently learned that 1959 was also the year the last surviving veteran of the United States Civil War died. How much change do you think he witnessed? Can you imagine seeing the advent of the airplane, telephone, electrification, the Great Depression, WWI, and WWII? I remember black and white television, rotary dial telephones, the moon landing, and the invention of personal computers, cell phones, and the Internet. Yet, for those of us who are old enough to remember, September 1, 1971 brought a change to the automobiles we drive on a daily basis.

No, it wasn't the invention of the automatic transmission, seat belts, power windows, or cruise control. What changed about driving was the design of the passenger side mirror. For a few years, automobile designers had dabbled with a convex mirror. A convex mirror gave drivers a wider field of view, which lessened the number of blind spots, which should have been a good thing. The problem? Things seen in that mirror were actually closer than they appeared. When a driver would glance in that mirror to see if the path of travel was clear, they would sometimes steer into the path of another vehicle, not realizing, until it was too late, how close they were to the vehicle in the mirror's reflection. Recognizing this potential for accidents, the Federal Motor Vehicle Safety Standards forced vehicle manufacturers to etch the now famous "Objects Are Closer Than They Appear" warning into each passenger side mirror.

Life is filled with things that are closer than they appear. I couldn't wait until I graduated from high school, and before I knew it, I was 25 years old with a wife and a daughter. April 14, 1980 marked the beginning of what is rapidly approaching a 40-year career with my employer. It seems like I barely blinked my eyes and my daughter went from a 2-year old blowing dandelion seeds to a 36-year old with 5-year old twins. I don't remember exactly when it happened, but one night, I went to sleep a young man and the next morning, I woke up OLD. If we could look in a mirror and see the lives we have lived, I'm sure there would be a warning that informed us, "Warning: The End Is Closer Than You Think."

It seems that life zips by at the speed of time. We all say that life is too short and if we could somehow just slow things down, we would gladly do so. We see our newborn child and before you know it, they seem to have outgrown us. The words, "Help me, Poppa," of my grandchildren have now become, "I can do it."

The end *is* closer than it appears. Matthew 24:36 tells us that no one knows when the end will be. Matthew 24:42 reminds us to remain alert and verse 44 tells us to be ready for the end. I would like to think that my personal end is years from now, but Proverbs 27:1 tells me not to worry about tomorrow because I don't know what today may bring. Since the end is closer that it appears, I may as well have the attitude found in Revelation, "He who testifies to these things says, 'Surely I am coming soon'" (Revelation 22:20a).

Eternal Savior. While I may not know when my end will come, I thank You that I am promised a home in heaven whenever that end arrives. Let me not spend a lifetime looking in the mirror at my past but let me look forward to the day of Your promised return. Amen.

> *Either make the tree good and its fruit good, or else make the tree corrupt and its fruit corrupt. For the tree is known by its fruit.* (Matthew 12:33)

KNOWING THE TREE

As a boy, I really enjoyed climbing trees. Between our house and my uncle's house was a stand of pine trees. These trees weren't super tall; they only averaged about 40 feet in height. Because boys will be boys, a couple of my childhood friends and myself would climb to the very top, break the top off, and climb back down. In our young brains, the act of climbing to the top and back without falling and breaking something other than the top of the tree somehow proved our bravery and worth as future men.

Flash forward a few years and I found myself working a job that managed electric utility rights-of-way. Part of the duties of that job required me to obtain a nationally recognized certification. To obtain this certification, one had to pass a very difficult test (passing being a minimum score of 80%) that required both experience and studying several reference manuals. Part of the test preparation included memorizing pictures and other characteristics (e.g., bark, leaves, needles, fruit, etc.) of 100 different trees found in the southeastern United States. I had to know these trees because 10 of the test questions came from those pictures and other information. Let's face it, when you have to score 80% on a 100-question test, you can't afford to throw away 10 questions. Would you believe the tree we call a red cedar is not really a cedar but a juniper? I didn't know that before the test but I do now. I had lived years thinking that a red cedar was a cedar tree because I was told it was a cedar tree.

We Christians are like trees. If you plant an apple seed, what are the odds you will produce a banana tree? Just as apple seeds produce apple trees, acorns produce oak trees, and sweet gum balls produce aggravation and bad thoughts (okay they produce sweet gum trees), we Christians are called to produce the fruits of God. According to Galatians, a Christian is called on to produce love, joy, peace, patience, kindness, goodness, faith, gentleness, and self-control. You may not think you have those seeds inside you, but if God wants us to produce those fruits, you can rest assured He gave each of us the seeds we need.

About that arborist test. Before I took the test, I was told that no one passes the test on their first attempt. I don't know if that person was using reverse psychology or not, but I took, *and passed*, that test. How did I pass a test on my first attempt that no one passes on their first attempt? Because I made up my mind that I would.

As far as passing God's test for planting fruit seeds, I'm still working on some of them. The way I look at it, if God expects me to plant a seed, the least I can do is go to the dirt.

Eternal Father. Thank You for the seeds You have given me to plant for Your kingdom. Remind me that You have tilled the soil; it is up to me to plant Your seeds. Amen.

The Lord shall fight for you, while you hold your peace.
(Exodus 14:14)

THE SMALLEST BATTLEFIELD

Gettysburg. Iwo Jima. Midway. Stalingrad. Northern Africa. Viet Nam. Normandy. Shiloh. The Ardennes Forest. These, and many, many more places stir up memories of bullets, knives, artillery shells, blood, life, and death. Many movies have been made and thousands of stories have been written that feature the sounds of war, stories of victory and defeat, and commands given to both "Charge!" and to retreat. Whether through endless planning and execution or blind luck, all wars are won or lost based on determination, preparation, and perseverance – or a lack of these.

In every battle, no matter how great or small, the will to win must replace the urge to surrender. Victory is rarely easy but must be claimed for the war to be won. Every battle ever waged was fought by hoards of men – and, to a lesser degree, women – who had the same goal, ultimate victory. All battlefields, regardless of their locations and the victor, are left littered with sweat, tears, and blood. And while every battlefield is unique, each has problems that must be overcome including swamps, hedgerows, trenches, hills, and other obstacles which, to the soldier fighting the fight, were just other things that had to be faced and defeated.

While world wars are famous for their heroes, there is a daily battle that each of us must fight. Our daily battles will never be made into a movie or a best-selling book. Our personal battlefield doesn't have rivers that must be crossed or hills that must be ascended, but our obstacles are no less real; doubt, fear, failure, loneliness, and rejection will attack from all angles. The battle that everyone, regardless of age, gender, status, ethnicity, or even the willingness to fight, must fight every day is not a battle for land or power but for the heart and soul.

Each day, Satan seeks to claim victory over our lives and each day, we must deflect Satan's charge. First Peter 5:8 warns us to be watchful and that our adversary, the devil, prowls around as a roaring lion, seeking out those to devour. We must prepare for each onslaught. We can close our eyes to the visual and plug our ears to the siren's song and think, "Finally, I can relax." Without fail, just about the time we exhale, we catch the scent of a new temptation as it wafts in from an unexpected front. We must remember that, just as God is our ever-present protector, Satan is our ever-present, never-ceasing tempter. And he never stops. Even after we have claimed eternal victory, he will not stop for he knows others are watching our actions and hearing our words. He may have lost the battle for *our* soul, but he knows there are many other souls out there just waiting to be claimed.

Our battle with temptation is not won with the firing of a weapon or the dodging of a bullet. Our battle with temptation is won day-by-day, overcoming one temptation at a time.

Heavenly Father. I pray You will point out Satan's attacks so I will not be broadsided and lose a battle I should have won. Show me the steps I should take, but, more importantly, those I should avoid in my daily walk through this battlefield for the soul. Amen.

For bodily exercise profits a little, but godliness is profitable in all things, holding promise for the present life and also for the life to come. (1 Timothy 4:8)

SPIRITUAL EXERCISE

Jack Lalanne, known by many as "the godfather of modern fitness," spent most of his life touting the benefits of physical exercise and proper nutrition. I'll admit it, I, like many others, need to exercise. Anyway, while researching the life of Mr. Lalanne, I found three quotes attributed to him that were particularly eye opening.

One: Jack claimed that he was here for the "here and now." He went on to say Billy Graham was here for the hereafter. Hmm. Two: Because he believed that a country's overall health depended on the health of its population, Lalanne referred to physical culture and nutrition as the "salvation of America." Double hmm. Finally: Sometime before his death, Mr. Lalanne supposedly said that he couldn't die because it would ruin his image. Turns out he was proven wrong on that one on January 23, 2011. One more hmm.

Some of us, Mr. Lalanne included, are preoccupied with creating and maintaining the so-called "perfect" image. Don't get me wrong, I'm not anti-exercise; I don't deny the benefits we can have by properly maintaining our bodies. After all, as a Christian, I believe the Bible when it tells me, "Do you not know that you are the temple of God, and that the Spirit of God dwells in you" (1 Corinthians 3:16). I also believe this: "What? Do you not know that your body is the temple of the Holy Spirit, who is in you, whom you have received from God, and that you are not on your own" (1 Corinthians 6:19).

There are many in our country who collectively spend billions of dollars and nearly that many hours doing cardio, lifting weights, and eating foods that are supposedly "good" for us. Again, all of that is great, but I wonder how many of us neglect the most important of all exercises? Many know that physical exercise may help us to live a little longer but how many know that spiritual exercise can help us live forever? Consuming the words of health magazines has, for many, replaced the eternal health found in the Bible. Many times, as I walk into the open doors of my church, I am passed by those who are jogging toward a perfect body but passing up on the perfection that is the salvation of Jesus (sorry Mr. Lalanne).

The goal of zero percent body fat is good, but it will never replace the goal that is 100% Christ-likeness. Physical exercise is fine, but we must not neglect the most important exercise of all, the exercise of the Spirit.

Eternal Father. Thank You for the body You have given me. I pray You will not only bless my physical body but the Spirit that You gave me when I became a Christian. Amen.

> *He who believes and is baptized will be saved. But he who does not believe will be condemned.* (Mark 16:16)

TWO TYPES OF PEOPLE

Years ago, I heard an old joke about the world having three different kinds of people, them who can count and them who can't. After telling it to a friend, they looked at me with a strange look, asking me about the third kind. "You only named two kinds. What's the third kind?" they asked. I just bowed my head, sighed, and walked away. It was then that I knew the two real kinds of people: those who get a joke and those who don't.

Male and female, short and tall, thin or not, friendly or mean, the list could continue over many pages. If I had the time and inclination, I could divide the people of the world into nice little groups. The fact is, other than the obvious differences between male and female (although some claim it's not that simple), we cannot be placed into neat little groups; we are simply too different. We speak different languages, have different occupations, live in different types of houses, and like different music and food. Despite some twins being identical, no two people are truly 100% the same.

But in some aspects, we can be grouped into either/or groups. If you are "with child," you're pregnant. If not, you're not; there is no such thing as being nearly pregnant. If your heart is beating, your lungs are breathing, and you have brain activity, you are alive, at least medically speaking. If none of those are happening, you are the opposite of alive, which is typically referred to as dead. And according to John 1:12, you are either a child of God or you are not.

We either have a soul that has been cleansed of sin or we have a soul that is still polluted, bound for hell. Either you have the Holy Spirit living within you or you don't. I may not be a mathematical genius but I can, despite what some may say, count to three. I don't know everything, but I do know that I've asked Jesus to take away my sins.

When it comes to eternity, you are either going to heaven or you are not. I've looked into both groups and I know which one I'm in. What about you?

Lord Jesus. Thank You for Your gift of salvation so that I, and all others who believe in You and have accepted that gift, can belong to God's eternal family. Amen.

> *But each man is tempted when he is drawn away by his own lust and enticed. Then, when lust has conceived, it brings forth sin; and when sin is finished, it brings forth death.*
> (James 1:14-15)

ROOTS AND ALL

When I first bought the house in which I now live, there was a Crepe Myrtle tree growing next to the front of the house. I know some people like to participate in aggressive pruning (A.K.A., "Crepe Murder") when it comes to Crepe Myrtle trees, but I don't believe in that, so I chose to allow this one to grow to its fullest potential. That is, until I realized the true extent of the tree's "fullest potential." There are miniature Crepe Myrtles and medium Crepe Myrtles and then there are full-sized Crepe Myrtles. Wanna guess which one I had? Yep, the biggun.

I was mowing the grass one day and I looked at that tree that had pretty much taken over one-third of the front of my house and decided that it had overstayed its welcome. So I grabbed a saw and started cutting just above ground level. After cutting the tree to the ground and pulling the trunk and few limbs to the curb, I took my drill and, after boring a few holes, poured a concoction that, I had been told, should kill the stump. The key word to that statement was "should."

After about three weeks, I noticed what appeared to be Crepe Myrtle shoots poking their little heads through the soil. "That can't be possible," I thought, "I poured that magic kill juice in the stump." After a minute or two, I determined that, yes, those shoots were indeed little bitty baby Crepe Myrtle trees and that simply wasn't going to work. After grabbing a shovel, I dug away the soil and discovered that my concoction had indeed killed the stump but it hadn't killed the roots.

Bad habits are like that. If we, who claim to be Christian, exhibit a lifestyle that states otherwise because of some habit – or habits – we aren't willing to kill, before long, the shoots of our bad habits will grow and diminish our Christian witness. When someone becomes a Christian, that someone must undergo a "roots and all" change in their lifestyle. Yes, God cleans us of our sins but the devil, more than anything, wants to constantly tempt you to return to your "old self." The Bible has many verses that emphasize "out with the old," but I think the best one can be found in the New Testament, "Therefore, if any man is in Christ, he is a new creature. Old things have passed away. Look, all things have become new" (2 Corinthians 5:17). If we reason that we will only do it "just once more," we are inviting that bad habit to take root and spread throughout our life.

When you ask God to point out something in your life that needs to be destroyed, be prepared to not only get rid of the visible but that part that you can't see. To make sure you kill the whole problem, sometimes you must be willing to move some dirt.

Lord Jesus. Thank You for forgiving me of my sins. I pray, Lord, You will continue to show me the things in my life that, if I let them, can grow to become a full-grown, witness-killing bad habit. Amen.

> *If it is possible, as much as it depends on you, live peaceably with all men.* (Romans 12:18)

GETTING INTO PRACTICE

Most of us have heard the expression, "Practice makes perfect." The meaning to that statement is to imply that the more you do something, the better at it you will be. You want to get so good that doing it becomes second nature; you do it without thinking. NASCAR may not immediately come to mind when you think of practice making perfect, but when you watch a top-tier pit crew apply their trade during the nearly twelve seconds it takes to change four tires, adjust the settings on a car, and empty nearly twenty gallons of fuel into the car's tank, you will witness the end result of thousands of hours of repeated practice.

As long as you are practicing something the correct way, you will most likely end up with a satisfactory result. Learn the correct way to bake a cake and you will have a tasty treat when all is said and done. Bake the cake the wrong way and your result will be an experiment that didn't quite work out. Experimenting with a cake is one thing but try working on an outboard motor without any practice and you will wind up with a bucket full of parts. Then you will be forced to take that motor and that bucket to someone who actually knows what they are doing because they have years of practice under their belt.

As a Christian, there are things we must practice. Prayer, studying our Bible, being thankful, forgiveness, and attending church services are understood to be a part of the Christian life. How about getting along with others? Some people are just naturally "people" people. They actually enjoy getting to know new people. Me? Nope, that is a learned skill that I am still working on. Being comfortable in a crowd of unfamiliar faces simply isn't one of my gifts. I still have to remind myself that, up until the moment I met her, my best friend was a stranger.

I have found that by making an effort, my comfort level with new groups has increased. During a conversation in one such group, the topic of getting along with others came up. Someone said something that really stuck with me; "We may as well get into practice of getting along because, when we get to heaven, we're going to be doing it for a long time."

A long time. That's one way of saying eternity. Rodney King, an man who was unknown by many prior to March 3, 1991, was forced into the spotlight during a turbulent time in our nation's history, once asked this question: "Can't we all just get along?" Just get along? If Mr. King were still alive, I would tell him yes, if we can find a way to put aside our petty differences and our pride and ask for God's help, I'm sure we can "just get along."

Lord God, I pray our country will see the benefits that are there for us if we turn from the things that divide us and give our attention to You. It is then, I'm sure, that we will find ourselves getting along like You originally intended. Amen.

> *And have embraced the new nature, which is renewed in knowledge after the image of Him who created it.*
> (Colossians 3:10)

A Face For Radio

Let's face it; most of us see only the external. Because we aren't God, we center our attention on appearances. And don't think the media in our life doesn't notice. Look at any television screen and what do you see? Youth – relatively speaking, striking physical appearances, perfectly aligned and bleached teeth, artist applied makeup and hairstyles, and smiles, smiles, and more smiles.

Imagine with me for a moment that you are listening to your favorite radio program or you are talking on the phone. If you don't know the person you are listening to, do you, like me, try to imagine what that person looks like? When you eventually meet that person, does your imagined face match their real face? I remember seeing a certain well-known political personality many times on television. When I actually did see the person in "real life," I was surprised to see he wasn't the towering person I had pictured. While the person of my imagination was well over six feet tall, the real man was what I would call diminutive in stature. I wasn't disappointed; I was reminded, yet again, that rarely does our imagination match the real thing.

Yes, the external – at least our impression of what the external should be – often influences our image of other people. As Christians, we read in Ephesians 5:1 that we are to be imitators of God. The world should see the Holy Spirit that lives within us. Although our exterior may not be what the world demands – young, wrinkle-free, toned, tanned, thin, and physically attractive – we can easily be the kind, compassionate, and caring servant Jesus calls us to be.

Just as it's likely for us to be surprised when we meet that once faceless owner of the voice we hear, we must constantly be aware that the world is looking for the blemish in our Christian life. When we become Christians, we are not to attempt to create some image we may think the world expects or wants; being a Christian means we are to be a living image of Christ who lives within us.

Nope, I'll never have a face or body for television, and I'm fine with that. What I do aspire to have is a heart that reflects and constantly seeks to please Jesus.

> *Lord in heaven. While my body may not be perfect according to the standards of this world, I know the forgiveness You have given me is perfect and that I have a perfect body waiting for me in my heavenly home. Amen.*

> *For freedom Christ freed us. Stand fast therefore and do not be entangled again with the yoke of bondage.* (Galatians 5:1)

END OF SENTENCE

Because I value my freedom, I've never come close to doing something that would result in going to jail if caught. Freedom is something most of us value. We live in a country that places our freedom above pretty much anything else. And because we live in a country that protects our freedoms, those freedoms can very easily be taken for granted. If there is no cost for the things you have been given, there is always the chance that those things may be easily forgotten.

No, I've never been inside an actual brick-and-mortar, bars-for-doors, lights-out-when-they-say-lights-out prison. But while I've not spent a single night behind those locked bars, I have known two men who spent a part of their lives on the bad side of the locked gate. Although we didn't talk too much about what they did to get in jail, we did discuss what they thought about while they were there.

If you were to sit down with either of them and ask how they spent their time, each of them will give you the same one word answer: thinking. Although they had committed different crimes, each has a similar story. Both spent time thinking about three separate but similar things. One: each of them thought about the things they had done that led to a life behind bars. Two: both of them developed a plan that would keep them out of jail once they were released. And three: while the other two items filled a lot of their time, nothing received more of their focus than did the day of their release. They each told me pretty much the same thing: once you lose your freedom, you want nothing else but to regain that which you lost.

We may not hear bars slam shut at night and we may not have someone tell us when to sleep and when to wake up, but each of us eventually finds ourselves inside the prison that is sin. The moment we commit our first sin, we are sentenced to an eternity that is suffering and separation from the freedom that is life with God. When we step behind those invisible bars, we relinquish any hope we had of being free to live the life God chose for us. Our release from that prison can only come from Jesus. Satan will never allow us to leave. Jesus must break us out.

All prisons are bad, some are quite terrible, but the prison of Hell has no earthly comparison. Hell is an eternal sentence from which there is no escape. Before we find ourselves there, we must plead our case before Jesus. We must confess our sins to Him and beg His forgiveness. Nothing less than that forgiveness will release us from our invisible cell. If we want true freedom, we must go through Jesus. Period. End of sentence.

My Savior in heaven. Thank You for the forgiveness freely given to any and all who ask for it. Remind us that the jail of hell has but one door, and whether or not we go through that door begins and ends with You. Amen.

> *He bears witness of what He has seen and heard, yet no one receives His testimony.* (John 3:32)

I DON'T BELIEVE YOU!

If you, like me, are a fan of the movie, *The Princess Bride*, when you hear the word, "Liar!" you can probably hear the high-pitched voice of the actress, Carol Kane, as she berates her movie husband, Miracle Max, for claiming the "mostly dead" hero said "to blathe." Many of us who like works of fiction such as movies, television shows, or books can probably name many of the characters and even quote their dialogue, but how many of us can recall the very real characters Yoshio Yamakawa and Tsuzuki Nakauchi? Not ringing a bell? Allow me a minute.

The battle with the Japanese empire during World War II was a grueling and ferocious military campaign against an enemy that was convinced it was destined to rule the world. The typical Japanese soldier was a true believer in every sense. Emperor Hirohito had convinced them that the world was theirs for the taking and all they had to do was take. Most Japanese soldiers honestly believed that no one could outmatch the force that was the Japanese military machine. Having said that, very few Japanese soldiers matched the dedication of Yamakawa and Nakauchi. These two were not only willing to fight to the end but to continue beyond that end.

Although Japan officially surrendered on September 2, 1945, these two remained hidden on a small island in the Philippines, holding out until, believe it or not, 2005. That's right. The final two holdouts from World War II hid for sixty years *after* the war ended. Why? They remained hidden because they feared that, if they returned to Japan, they would be court-martialed for failure to perform their duty. They simply refused to believe that Japan's goal of world domination was not meant to be.

Because Jesus had come from heaven, He had seen miracles and wonders that were beyond the ability of human imagination. Today, as in Jesus' time, many simply refuse to believe. Many in Jesus' time refused to believe He was who He said He was and many today refuse to believe a place like heaven exists. Some don't believe in God; others don't believe in eternal reward or punishment; and others, while they believe in sin, cannot believe that they can receive forgiveness for those sins. The old adage "some things never change" still lives in the minds and hearts of those who refuse to believe something when the evidence suggests otherwise.

According to history, the earth was once thought to be flat, then it was thought that the earth was the center of the universe, and, finally, some will tell you that this thing we call life happened simply because of some huge accident. God gave each of us the freedom to believe – or not. We can choose to surrender or to hold out. Despite their fears, Yamakawa and Nakauchi were able to go home. They fought their war long after it was over. Your war has been won. Claim the victory and come home.

Lord Jesus, thank You for fighting the war I couldn't win. Thank You for the freedom that comes with surrender. I choose to believe in You. Amen.

> *When many of the Jews learned that He was there, they came, not for Jesus' sake only, but that they might also see Lazarus, whom He had raised from the dead. So the chief priests planned to put Lazarus to death also, because on account of him many of the Jews went away and believed in Jesus.*
> (John 12:9-11)

THE CROWD YOU RUN WITH

Who hasn't heard the phrase, "Guilty by association"? We all have groups of people with whom we associate. Having worked for more than forty years at the same company, I am constantly reminding new employees that Alabama Power Company is not just a name on a shirt; it's who they are. If you are a fan of one of the two major college football programs in the State of Alabama, you are either a "Bammer" or an "Aubie." Because I'm a fan of Kyle Busch, I'm a member of "Rowdy Nation." In some circles, gun owners are referred to as "gun nuts"; others call them "well-prepared individuals."

We all belong to different groups. As long as those groups mean no harm, no harm will come from being a part of them. Right now, I'm a member of a Facebook group, the *Bass Cat Owners Group*. I'll bet you can guess what the members of that group have in common. When this life is over, we won't be judged by which team we pulled for or which NASCAR driver we followed, or which kind of fishing boat we owned. We won't even be judged by what church we were a member of or how many Bible study groups we participated in.

When our lives on this earth are over, the next group you will join depends on how you answer this question: "Are you a Christian?" Your good deeds will not be questioned nor will your charitable donations. Your donations of time and money to God's causes – while they are appreciated – won't amount to the proverbial "hill of beans" when it comes to membership in your eternal group. A ragged Bible filled with notes and underlined scriptures is a good source of how to live but it isn't your room key to your heavenly home.

All of these, and many more, are worthwhile endeavors, but the only thing that will matter is how you answer that single question: "Are you a Christian?" Answer yes and all of those other things will be noted. But if you want an eternity of regret, just say, "No." I can promise you one thing: of all the groups there are, that's the one group you don't want to hang out with.

Eternal Father. Thank You for guiding me and telling me which crowd You want me to run with. I pray You will continue to guide my steps and keep me on Your path. Amen.

> *Be strong and of a good courage. Fear not, nor be afraid of them, for the Lord your God, it is He who goes with you. He will not fail you, nor forsake you.* (Deuteronomy 31:6)

YOUR SAFETY NET

It's been years since I attended a circus. I remember as a young boy seeing the lights, the animals (lions, tigers, and lest I forget, elephants), the clowns, jugglers, and impossibly tall men taking unimaginably long steps as they paraded throughout the covered arena. Those were great, but the act that made the deepest impression on me was the people who seemed to fly through the air high above the center ring.

To my young mind, there seemed to be some sort of magic that allowed both the male and female performers (likely named *The Flying Gambinos* or something like that) to soar above the ring, held in place by two impossibly thin steel cables, a crossbar, and nerves made from the same steel as the cables that suspended them. As one of the young men would dangle from the swinging bar, only the muscles in his legs preventing him from tumbling to the earth, one of the female artists would release her grip from her bar, fly through the air, and stop her fall by grabbing the hands of her upside down partner.

After flying to and fro for several minutes, the performers would, one-at-a-time, release their grip from the relative safety of the steel bar and fall to the ground. Here's the good part, they never hit the ground, at least during their fall. This was the time that the single most important part of their equipment came into play. A huge safety net, suspended under the flying team the entire time, caught and gently slowed each of the falling performers, preventing serious injury or perhaps death. After the net had stopped bouncing, each member of the no-longer *Flying Gambinos* would roll to the edge, grasp the edge, and, after a well-timed flip, step to the ground, take their bows, and prepare for their next performance.

Life is like that. All of us want some kind of assurance that, should we stumble or get tripped up by our bad decisions, there will be a safety net preventing us from falling to our destruction. When it comes to eternity, too many people are flying through life with no safety net in place to catch them or to prevent them from falling to an everlasting doom. If we leave this life without the safety that God provides, there will be no net to prevent our eternal fall. It is only God's safety net – His free gift of salvation and the forgiveness of our sins – that can save us from an eternity of death and separation from Him. It is only through our faith in that net that we can be guaranteed a safe landing whenever that fall occurs.

In today's society, there are daredevils who want to experience an adrenalin rush in practically everything they do. For them, safety nets are for the weak. I look at it a different way; before I swing from the heights, I want to know that God will be there to catch me when I come tumbling down.

My God and my Redeemer. Although some prefer to face life, and the eternity after it, without the security of the safety net that is Your salvation, I am thankful You will be there to provide a soft landing when my fall from this life occurs. Amen.

> *O Lord, in the morning You will hear my voice; in the morning I will direct my prayer to You, and I will watch expectantly.*
> (Psalm 5:3)

OFF ON A GOOD NOTE

Have you ever had a day that started off on the proverbial wrong foot? Perhaps you woke up on the wrong side of the bed. I know I have. From time to time, we all have one of "those days." Let's say you have an early meeting at work so you set your alarm to jar you from your restful sleep thirty minutes earlier than normal. The only problem, you set the alarm time but you didn't turn on the alarm's buzzer. You wake from your slumber and realize that you have over-slept. Not by much, so if you hurry you can still make the meeting. At least you set the coffee pot to be ready when you rose from your bed.

You quickly dress. Grabbing a shirt, you frown as the button you have been telling yourself to re-sew finally falls to the floor. Not the end of the world; you grab another. Fine. You enter the kitchen, wondering why the coffee pot is not finished. Then you see it; you never flipped the switch for the timer. You then switch the pot to brew and gather your things and put them into the car. After a couple of minutes, you pour your coffee into your travel mug and head for the door.

You push the button to start the car and you hear it, or rather, you don't hear it. The motor doesn't start! Dead battery! After a second, you realize you never grabbed your key – it's still on the counter – by your phone. You dash back into the house, grab the key and the phone and check your watch. As long as traffic cooperates, you'll make it with a couple of minutes to spare. You start the car, back into the street, then you have that nagging feeling that something is missing. What could it be? The report you worked on last night? It's still beside your computer in your home office.

And so it goes. An entire morning filled with starts and stops, stops and starts. Even when we are having one of "those mornings," do we ever take time to thank God for the gift of the day? Do we ever ask Him to bless whatever it is we are about to do? Do we ask Him to bless those we will meet throughout the day? Do we pray that He will bless our efforts and that those efforts will bring honor to Him? How about asking for safe travels for both ourselves and those with whom we share the road?

The Bible tells us to "Rejoice always. Pray without ceasing. In everything give thanks, for this is the will of God in Christ Jesus concerning you" (1 Thessalonians 5:16-18). We enjoy the coffee but do we thank Him who gave us the coffee, the cream, the water, the sugar, the cup, the spoon, and the coffee pot?

The next time you find yourself having one of "those days," or any other day, take a few seconds to offer a word or two of thanks. Even when we are having that day, remember, our best day could be just around the corner and our best beginning may just be right now.

Heavenly Father. Thank You for the gift that is every day. When I am having one of "those days," let me not get caught up in my temporary problems but remind me of Your promised eternal reward. Amen.

> So Abram departed, as the Lord had spoken to him, and Lot went with him. Abram was seventy-five years old when he departed from Harran. (Genesis 12:4)

SPINNERS

It seems that everywhere you turn, you see an accessorized car or truck. From mega-watt sound systems to LED lighting to custom paint jobs to "jacked-up" four-wheel drive pickups to multi-spoke 26" (or higher) chrome wheels, it seems that some people want their ride to reflect their unique personality. Several years ago, as I sat in my stock vehicle, something caught my eye from an older Chevrolet Impala that had come to a stop beside me. Curious, I turned and I saw that a part of the stopped car's wheels was still rotating. "That's weird," I thought. "How in the world . . . ?" Such was my introduction to spinners.

If you've never seen a spinner, it's a custom wheel with an outer disc that rotates pretty much at its own speed. The disc can continue to spin when the car comes to a stop or not spin at all as the car proceeds down the highway. Whoever came up with the design of spinners intended to catch your eye. I'll admit it; they certainly caught mine.

After thinking about the wheel within the wheel (nope, not like the ones Ezekiel saw), I began to wonder, am I a spinner? I'll admit that I like things at my own pace but I'm talking about someone who does their own thing at their own speed. If I'm talking about trying to keep pace with the world, then my own pace is probably a good thing, but suppose God wants me to move at His pace and I want to do things the way I want to do them?

God doesn't want spinners. God wants us to move at the pace He chooses when He chooses. Abram was, by our standards, an old man when God called him to take all he had, leave his homeland, and go to a "To Be Determined" location. According to the Genesis account, Abram didn't wait around. He didn't tell God that he would get to that when he felt like it. And he certainly didn't sit there and spin without getting anything accomplished.

Yeah, spinners are unique. They catch the eye when first seen. But spinners are meant to do their own thing. If I find myself spinning away but nothing seems to be happening, I probably need to get on pace with God and His plan. I certainly don't want to catch His eye because I'm moving a lot but not getting anything accomplished.

Heavenly Father. If You see me spinning at my own speed and not making any progress, take the spinners from my life and give me the wheels You intended me to have. Amen.

> *Let no unwholesome word proceed out of your mouth, but only that which is good for building up, that it may give grace to the listeners.* (Ephesians 4:29)

BUT

If you are old enough, you may remember the television game show, *Name That Tune*. The premise of the game was simple enough; a contestant had to identify a song's name after hearing only a few notes of the song without the benefit of lyrics. Prior to the actual naming of the tune, the two contestants played a quick bidding game. One contestant would declare they could name the tune in so many notes (we'll say, five). The process continued with fewer and fewer notes until one opponent challenged the other to "Name that tune!" Some contestants were so sure of their musical identification ability, that, after hearing a clue about the song, they would claim they could name the tune after hearing only a single note. Talk about confidence.

How about this? You are involved in a game called "Kill That Dream." The object: the winning bidder has to kill the dream of the opponent using as few words as possible. I, having the advantage of knowing your dream, claim I can kill your dream by using only a single word. You see, this little three-letter, single-syllable word has, over the years, killed the dreams of thousands, if not millions of people. Aspirations have been wiped out, passions doused, ambitions smothered, and happiness extinguished at the mere mention of this all too common word.

"Dad!" shouted the young fellow, "did you see my hit?"

"Mom!" she excitedly said to her mother, "I scored 99 on my final!"

"Sweetheart!" the young woman informed her husband, "I got the interview!"

"Hey, dear," said the husband as he opened the door, tired after a long week at work, "I remembered your cleaning."

All of these people have something good to say or have just achieved a goal they have been trying to reach for quite a while. Each of these, in their private thoughts, want to share their success with someone they look up to or share their life with.

"I saw it, son," said dad, "but we've really got to work on those strikeouts."

"That's great," said mom, "but wouldn't 100 have been better?"

"That's good news," said the husband, "but this is the third interview this month."

"That's great, hon," she said, "but now we're going to be late for dinner with the neighbors."

But.

As parents, husbands, wives, co-workers, teachers, or whatever we are to others, we all have opportunities to build up or tear down. When presented with an opportunity to either encourage or discourage, we must always seek an opportunity to help and not hinder.

The Israelites, after having been slaves for hundreds of years, were finally free of their harsh Egyptian masters. After being led by God from captivity, the Hebrews now found themselves on the banks of the Red Sea, seemingly trapped as Pharaoh's army was rushing toward them, ready to put the people of Israel back in line. Seeing only the wide expanse of water before them, the people cried to Moses, telling him that he had doomed them to destruction.

I can imagine Moses reminding them that God had not delivered them this far just to turn them back over to the Egyptians. "That's great, Moses," they complained, "BUT now we are trapped here. It would have been better had we remained in Egypt." If you are familiar with Exodus 14:5-31, you know how this story ends. Even after their miraculous delivery through the parted Red Sea, the people quickly found other "Buts" to voice. "But, Moses, we're hungry." "But, Moses, we're thirsty." "But, Moses, we're tired of manna; we want some meat."

It's easy to "but" someone's dream. In most cases, yes, there will always be a higher goal to aim for or a bigger success to celebrate. But since today is all we have, can we not just celebrate the win of today? "That was a great hit, son. Let's grab an ice cream." See how easy that was?

Eternal God. I'm thankful You are there to celebrate each of my victories as they happen, no matter how insignificant they may seem to others, You let me know You are pleased when I serve You and Your will. With You, there is no "But"; with You, there is only "Here, let Me help you with that." Amen.

> *The pride of your heart has deceived you, you who live in the clefts of the rock, whose dwelling is high; you say in your heart, "Who will bring me down to the ground?" Though you ascend high like the eagle, and though you set your nest among the stars, I will bring you down from there, says the Lord.*
> (Obadiah 1:3-4)

AT LEAST I'M NOT...

Pride is such a simple word. We all know someone who is a living billboard for pride. We cringe when we see them. You haven't even heard a word from them and yet, you know what you will hear. "Did you hear," she may ask, "that my husband finally got that big promotion? It's about time we were able to leave this neighborhood with the people who have been moving in." Subtle. Then she looks your way and affirms she wasn't talking about you. "Present company excluded, of course." Thanks.

His grin reveals his newly bleached and perfectly straight teeth. As he puts his hand on your shoulder, he tells you, "I know, I've seen that look in your eye. You're thinking that, someday, you want to be like me. Everyone needs aspirations but sometimes, we have to look in the mirror and realize we're doing the best we can." Real class act, that guy. These are fictitious examples but recent news reports reveal that many of today's youths refuse to work a job they feel is "beneath" them.

Pride is easy. Knowing you are prideful is the hard part. We see others and we think it's okay to be a little prideful when you've finally arrived. We can even be proud of the fact that we think we aren't prideful. The good doctor Luke tells us what Jesus said about being prideful when He talked about two men and how they prayed.

A Pharisee and a tax collector enter the temple. The Pharisee, because he was used to his position in the temple, stood as he prayed. He thanked God that he was not like other men; men who steal, cheat, or practice adultery. He even reminded God – in case God had overlooked it – that he fasted not once but two times – EACH WEEK! Knowing the tax collector was within earshot, he also thanked God that he wasn't like him, a lowly tax collector. The tax collector stood at a distance; he didn't look upward because he knew he wasn't worthy. His anguish was apparent as he simply asked for God's mercy because he knew he was a sinner. According to Jesus, the tax collector was the one who went home right with God. Jesus concluded the story with this: "For everyone who exalts himself will be humbled, and he who humbles himself will be exalted" (Luke 18:14b).

The Pharisee never said he was prideful, he just said he was glad that he wasn't as bad as others. It's easy for us to say, "Yeah? Well at least I'm not as bad as [enter name here]." Pride won't allow humility to take root. Only by bowing our head in humility will we break the back of that thing called pride.

Father God in heaven. The next time I am tempted to be prideful of something I did or said or even thought, remind me it's not pride You want but humility. Amen.

> *Whoever comes to Me and hears My words and does them, I will show whom he is like: He is like a man who built a house, and dug deep, and laid the foundation on rock. When the flood arose, the stream beat vehemently against that house, but could not shake it, for it was founded on rock.* (Luke 6:47-48)

FOUNDATION OR FAÇADE?

Today's modern architecture is quite amazing. A building can be constructed to resemble pretty much anything. With enough money and time, you can live in anything from Cinderella's castle to The White House or pretty much anything in between. Aesthetics – the way something looks – seems to always be on the mind of the architect. From the buildings we work in to the signs we see, the aesthetics must be pleasing to the eye.

In real life, the part of those buildings we see is only a thin veneer of what the building actually is. What we see is a façade, a false face. The foundation and the inner layout determine what the building actually is. If the building doesn't have a solid foundation and a well-built internal structure, it won't be much of a building after only a few stresses and storms.

People are the same way. Some people spend countless hours and many dollars constantly constructing their façade. They want the world to see a youthful or a fresh face. As we age and face the storms of life, it's not our external façade but our internal foundation that will sustain us. A life that depends more on the façade of the world than the foundation of Jesus is like a man who builds his house on a foundation of sand. "But he who hears and does not obey is like a man who built a house on the ground without a foundation, against which the stream beat vehemently. Immediately it fell, and the ruin of that house was great" (Luke 6:49).

Do we worry more about the face we put on for the world or do we spend more time making sure our foundation is well cared for? Spending time with God – reading His Word, praying, asking Him to strengthen our weaknesses – will ensure we have that solid foundation. Yes, the world may tell us to put our best face forward and we must present a pleasing façade for all to see. We can listen to the world or we can make sure we spend time with the Master Builder in order that our foundation will pass His test.

God in heaven. I pray You will continue to point out the things I need to work on to make sure my foundation is one that will meet Your standards. Amen.

> *Every branch in Me that bears no fruit, He takes away. And every branch that bears fruit, He prunes, that it may bear more fruit. (John 15:2)*

PRUNING FOR EFFECT

When it comes to horticulture, pruning is the process of cutting away branches that are neither wanted, essential, needed, or desirable. Pruning is sometimes necessary to form a healthier or more visually appealing tree. Some have turned creative pruning into an art form better know as topiary or Bonsai. Whatever you call it, from time-to-time, some trees need to be pruned. I have several Japanese maples scattered around my yard. One, a green leafed variety called Viridis, was in dire need of some selective pruning. It had grown from the miniature tree I desired into something of a wild shrub. After about a half-hour of snipping here and there, I stepped back and took stock of my work. "Perfect," thought I, "just what I wanted." Now, more than two years later, the tree still has the look I wanted when it was first purchased.

Have you ever wondered why farmers annually prune the limbs from fruit trees? Pruning allows sunlight and rain better access to the center of the tree and increases air circulation through the branches. It also encourages the tree to produce fresh shoots, which produce more fruit. After all, dead branches will never produce fruit. And a peach tree that doesn't produce peaches is nothing more than wasted space in an orchard.

Let's face it, from time-to-time; we all need to prune the clutter from our lives. If you are like me, the kitchen countertop is where I toss my daily mail. I'll separate the important things from the junk, telling myself I'll toss it later. Before I know it, part of that countertop has disappeared under a stack of sales papers or letters from realtors who want to buy my house or credit card offers promising everything but the moon. And don't get me started about my garage. While I still have ample space to park my vehicle, over time, the other half has become a collection area for miscellaneous and assorted stuff.

Our lives are like those trees, my countertop, or my garage. Over time, we collect bad habits or excuses as to why we don't have time to do the things that need doing. Our days are filled with work, which is necessary, and our evenings are filled with empty entertainment instead of healthy items such as reading Scripture or prayer or time alone with God. James 4:8 tells me that if I draw near to God, He will draw near to me. If my life is cluttered with unnecessary or dying things, how can I expect to bear the fruit necessary to have a life filled with the spirit of God?

That maple looked better after being pruned. My countertop and garage better serve their purpose when I clean the junk from them. And I find that when I prune the junk from my life, I am able to bear more and better fruit for God.

Eternal Father. Thank You for sending Your Holy Spirit to fill my life. Let me not collect so much of the world's junk that I am unable to bear the fruit You would have me bear. Amen.

> *There, two blind men sitting by the road, when they heard that Jesus was passing by, cried out, "Have mercy on us, O Lord, Son of David!" The crowd rebuked them, that they should be silent. But they cried out even more, "Have mercy on us, O Lord, Son of David!" Jesus stood still and called to them, saying, "What do you want Me to do for you?" They said to Him, "Lord, let our eyes be opened."* (Matthew 20:30-33)

THE SQUEAKY WHEEL

There are two sayings about the proverbial squeaky wheel: (1) squeaky wheels get greased, or (2) squeaky wheels get replaced. Squeaky wheels, we all have them. From time-to-time, the bearings on my boat trailer have to be packed with grease. Without the periodic application of grease, those bearings will have to be replaced. Over time, parts, components, what-cha-ma-call-its, thing-a-ma-jigs, hickey-doos, and doo-flatchies (each of these is real, ask any man) need attention.

I have a small refrigerator in my office. It's not that old but it has started to make a weird noise when it does its cooling thing. It still works, but eventually, it will have to be replaced. On the other hand, if the motor on my boat starts acting up, it is going to need repairs. When I show up at the shop, the first thing I'm going to do is tell the mechanic what the motor is doing. But suppose I take my boat to the shop and leave without communicating the problem. Should I be surprised if it doesn't get fixed? If I don't talk to the mechanic, he won't know where to start.

The story of the two blind men from Matthew reminds me of this. Imagine if you were one of the blind men. Somehow you had learned that Jesus could perform miracles including, of all things, restoring sight to the blind. It just so happens that you are blind and it also just so happens that Jesus is coming through your little corner of the world. Would you quietly sit there, hoping that Jesus would read your thoughts? Or would you shout from the top of your lungs, "JESUS! HELP ME!" And when the crowd turned and told you, "Hush, blind man. Shut your mouth!" would you shrink back against your wall, ashamed that you had somehow disturbed the proceedings? These two didn't "hush," and I have a feeling neither would you.

When your car's battery is giving you trouble, you don't tell the mechanic the windshield washer fluid is low. When you are hungry and at a restaurant, you don't ask for a recipe to make bread. When Jesus asked these men, "What do you want Me to do for you?" they didn't cower or mumble, they told Jesus exactly what they wanted. Those two wanted one thing and one thing only. They wanted to see. "Open our eyes!"

When we pray to Jesus and we have a specific need, Jesus wants us to voice that need. Yes, God knows our needs, but He wants us to have the faith to let Him know what it is. If you're going to be a squeaky wheel, (1) make sure you are heard, and (2) make sure you're being heard by the One who can fix you.

Eternal Father. I know every time I come to You in prayer, it seems I have something in my life needing to be fixed. I thank You that You have answered my prayer so many times. And for the things still needing attention, grant me the faith to know You are working on those, in Your own time. Amen.

Not serving when eyes are on you, but as pleasing men as the servants of Christ, doing the will of God from the heart.
(Ephesians 6:6)

WHY WORK?

Four twenty-five a.m. Pretty much every day, Monday through Friday, long before the sun peeks over the Eastern horizon, my alarm clock sounds the first of two sleep-breaking calls. Why in the world would any sane person set a clock to intentionally wake them up at such an early hour? In a single word: work. I have to go to work. Anyone who's ever answered that call will tell you the same thing; they *must* work.

Thinking about it, do I really have to go to work? Well, if I want to continue living in my house and driving my car and eating the food I want to eat and have access to the Internet and do the other things I do, yes, I have to go to work. To get paid money, I must work. My employer and I have an agreement; they agree to pay me a set amount of money in exchange for a satisfactory amount of my labor. Do I enjoy my job? For the most part, yes, my job provides other rewards in addition to the aforementioned money. But why do I work?

As a Christian, I am instructed that everything I do must be done to bring glory to God. I am to do all things always seeking an opportunity to show the world that, first and foremost, I serve God. I work to serve others. My job revolves around helping others so they can work as safely as they can.

God has given me a certain number of gifts and talents. My job is to ensure I use those gifts and talents not only to satisfy my employer but also to bring glory and honor to God. I enjoy my job, but if my job requires me to do something that forces me to compromise my faith, I must remember that my service to God must always come first.

Each morning, when I rise from my very comfortable bed and splash some water on my still sleepy face, I look in the mirror and wonder how much longer I plan on doing this. It's been a long forty years and the end of my earthly career is growing nearer every day. But when it comes to my working for God, I can find nowhere in the Bible that tells me it's okay to quit doing God's work.

Never-Ending Father. Thank You for the talents and other gifts that enable me to perform my job to the best of my ability. I pray that my efforts to bring glory to You through the work I do are pleasing to You. Amen.

He must increase, but I must decrease.
(John 3:30)

A First Place Christian

There was a time that I was obsessed with following certain sports. I had computer spreadsheets of statistics and trends. I read article after article – first from magazines then from the Internet – to ensure I had all the information I needed. "Why," you may be wondering, "would someone spend so much time over something that is, in the end, just a game?" After some time, God and I had a talk and He showed me that my obsession had become an idol. It was then that I quickly reduced my involvement to that of a casual fan.

Don't get me wrong, I still enjoy some sports, NASCAR and professional fishing being the two primary sports I follow. I can hear you now, saying that neither of those are sports. We'll have to agree to disagree. Anyway, the one thing about professional sports that turns me off is the lifestyles of many of today's modern athletes. From the outlandish way they decorate their bodies to the "me, me, me" their actions and words portray, it seems our modern society expects the "me above all others" attitude (the one that is discouraged in the Bible) that a lot of athletes are only happy to oblige.

When it comes to being first, we can find instances of this in all walks of life, from sport (with some, this begins in little league, if not earlier) to business to school to cooking and, as sad as it is to say, even in church. No matter the activity, there are some people in every venture who are more than willing to toot their own horn. According to his third book, John specifically mentions a man by the name of Diotrephes, "I wrote to the church, but Diotrephes, who loves to put himself first among them, but did not accept us" (3 John 9). Sadly, the attitude that was apparent nearly two thousand years ago still lives with some today.

There have been occasions that opportunistic Christians have been more than willing to point out to me that the version of the Bible I carry is the wrong version. When I am told that there is only "ONE TRUE BIBLE," and that "ALL OTHER VERSIONS FALL SHORT," I find myself thinking, "That's strange. I don't recall reading anywhere that Jesus read His Aramaic translation of the King James Version. Musta missed that."

When it comes to traditions, especially those associated with the church, those traditions must be tested with a single question: "Is it Biblical"? Just as Christians must compare ourselves to one standard – the teachings of Jesus – our traditions and teachings must either survive or die because of God's Word and the words of His Son.

When it comes to my place as a Christian, I must always yield to the One who's name is first among CHRISTians. Jesus was, is, and always will be FIRST.

Christ Jesus. When I am tempted to think of myself before You, remind me that without You, there is no Christian for me to be. Amen.

> *When He had called the people to Him, with His disciples, He said to them, "If any man would come after Me, let him deny himself and take up his cross and follow Me. For whoever would save his life will lose it. But whoever would lose his life for My sake and the gospel's will save it."* (Mark 8:34-35)

CHICKEN OR A PIG?

When someone sits down to enjoy a good old-fashioned country breakfast, two components of the meal absolutely must be, as I am prone to say, absotively, posilutely present or it's not a real country breakfast. And what would those vital components be? Eggs, either scrambled or fried – for me, both have to be well-done, no runny yellow for me – and either bacon, sausage, or ham, if not all three. Without those ingredients, the rest of the meal is somehow lacking. There's an old adage about breakfast that goes something like this: The chicken participates but the pig, he's committed.

When someone takes part in an endeavor, either they participate in, or they are committed to, the project. When a husband and a wife decide they want to have a child, the husband gets to participate but it's the wife who is committed. The husband was there during the conception but, after that, he is more-or-less just along for the ride. He may try to understand what his wife is going through, but he can never truly comprehend all of the changes his wife must endure. And while the husband participates, the wife is committed to the entire process, from beginning to end. She goes through hormonal changes, physical changes, and general life changes for the entire nine months.

Based on my observances, the same level of involvement can be applied to Christianity. There are those who want to participate and there are those who are fully committed to the Christian life. Participants attend church as long as it isn't too inconvenient. They will sit patiently through the sermon and nod at the appropriate times. Their Bible should last a while because it rarely gets opened. Prayer is that "break glass in case of emergency" Christian tool that is occasionally used, if the need should arise. The participant will tell you the reason they don't give thanks for their meal is that God knows that they are thankful for everything so why waste time telling God something He already knows?

The committed Christian will be at church not because it's the right thing to do but because they don't feel right if they don't. They have a well-worn Bible that's filled with underlined passages and notes in the margins. Their knees know the posture of prayer and their necks understand the bow of the humble. Committed Christians find it strange not to give thanks for their food but they don't judge those who choose otherwise.

Jesus was committed to the will of His Father as He prayed for strength in the garden. As Peter drew his sword to defend Jesus on the night of His betrayal and arrest, Jesus reminded Peter that God would spare Him should Jesus choose to ask, "Do you think I cannot now pray to My Father, and He will at once give Me more than twelve legions of angels" (Matthew 26:53). But Jesus was committed to God's plan for our salvation, even up to His death on the cross.

Back to the breakfast, the chicken is a willing participant through the gift of the eggs. But the pig, he's the committed one. When it comes to the Christian life, are you a chicken or are you a pig?

Lord Jesus. If there ever comes a time I have to make a decision on being a participant or being committed to You, I pray I would have the strength, courage, and conviction to play the part of the pig instead of the chicken. Amen.

> *The Lord is near to the broken-hearted, and saves the contrite of spirit.* (Psalm 34:18)

IF IT AIN'T BROKE...

I was looking through my house earlier this week and realized that I have a few things that are, in this world of materialism we live in, old. My coffee maker, mattress, and television are 13 years old. I'm guessing in object years, that makes them, I don't know, probably somewhere close to being obsolete. As I write this story on the Saturday after Thanksgiving, yesterday, being the unofficial national holiday of consumerism – a.k.a. "Black Friday" – I was reminded via all sorts of media, that I should replace all those things in my house that are older than, say, two weeks. And I'll admit, there are times I have been tempted by the new, the improved, and the better than ever before.

Technology, with all of its advancements, sometimes forces us to replace something simply because it is no longer supported. Even the computer that I am using to type this story, according to Apple, by now, should have been replaced not once but at least twice. One of these days, I know I will have to replace it, but, more and more, I find myself falling into the category of, "if it ain't broke, why replace it?"

People are like that. I'm sure most of us know someone who has an issue or two. I don't have to go far before I see one of those people. Less than 20 steps from the chair on which I am sitting is a full-length mirror. When I open that closet door, I see someone who has quite a number of gray hairs. My jeans seem to be getting tighter, not because of their shrinkage but because of my growage. I've determined that we need to quit looking at wrinkles as something to be hidden; I say let them be seen. And there was a time in my life that the simple task of rising from my bed each morning was accomplished without sound effects.

I've been told that the goal of the United States Marine Corps is to first break down a new recruit so they can then mold him or her into the honed and toned fighting force needed to face whatever foe that needs to be defeated. Some think God does the same. But God doesn't break us down; we do a fine job of that without His help. It is only when we admit we are broken – because of sin – that we can begin the journey required to be fixed.

Sadly, there are those who believe they can fix themselves. They don't realize that doing good is not what it takes to fix their problem. Good works and deeds are great but they must come as a result of a repaired heart, not as an effort to make the repair. Self-repair is a small bandage on a wound that needs major surgery, and the only thing this bandage will do is guarantee an eternity of suffering and remorse. It is only after we come to God, admitting our brokenness and that we aren't worthy of repair, that God can mend the un-mendable.

There are things that we can fix and there are things we can replace. Only God can fix the one thing that can't be found in a store or on a website. Souls aren't buy one get one. And there is no soul that is so broken that God can't fix.

Eternal Father. Thank You for fixing the unfixable and forgiving the unforgivable. Amen

> *For our fight is not against flesh and blood, but against principalities, against powers, against the rulers of the darkness of this world, and against spiritual forces of evil in the heavenly places.* (Ephesians 6:12)

BEHIND ENEMY LINES

World War II, Normandy, France. Close to 13,000 American paratroopers had been dropped behind enemy lines under the cover of darkness. In the confusion of war, they were dropped in locations other than those planned. Some were shot as they floated toward earth; others died as they landed. Those that survived faced a harrowing situation. It was dark and they were in an unfamiliar land. They couldn't call out to others because to talk meant being heard and being heard meant possible death. Their maps were nearly useless because using a flashlight created the possibility of exposing yourself to the enemy risking not only your life but perhaps those of your unit.

Reading historical accounts of these brave men tells me I don't envy their plight. They were cut off from their team, surrounded by the enemy, and unsure whether to go forward or to retreat. They didn't know whether to turn left or right or simply hunker down where they were. Some had been injured upon their landing, but of those who survived, most were sound. Weapons had been lost and those with radios understandably hesitated to use them. They didn't know if they were miles from the enemy or within earshot of their German foe. Being alone behind enemy lines is not a situation most warriors relish, but it's a possibility for which all must prepare.

We Christians may wake up each morning in our bed, sheltered by our familiar house, drink coffee in our kitchen, and drive to work on roads we know in the vehicle we own. While all of this may seem like friendly territory, we are behind the lines of an ancient enemy. This enemy has unimaginable weapons of warfare at his disposal and he has no compunction when it comes to using them. In his effort to defeat us, he will show no mercy and his devious plans seem to know no end. The shadows are his friend; each corner may find him lurking, waiting to pounce at the slightest sign of weakness on our part. He will devour us without hesitation, given a hint of an opportunity.

There is no man-made defense, modern or ancient, that he has not seen and overcome. We cannot afford to leave our homes without wearing the armor of God that will protect us. Our so-called "safe spaces" are no match for him. Lock our doors and windows to keep him at bay? Who are we kidding? Copper wires and broadband signals are his preferred mode of entry into our modern world. PG ratings? Have you really watched a PG movie lately? Our enemy has never been more powerful while being so invisible than he is today.

Are we behind enemy lines? Yes we are. But we are not alone. Jesus has travelled the same battlefield. He and He alone has defeated this enemy. Jesus won then and, with His help, we can win now. Despite the haze of our present battle, the thing we must remember is this: in the end, we win.

Dear Jesus. Help me recognize that, while this may seem to be friendly terrain to me, I am in the territory of the enemy. Protect me from his attacks and provide me with the strength and courage I need to overcome whatever he throws my way.
Amen.

> *And he sought after God in the days of Zechariah, the one who instructed him in the fear of the Lord. And in the days that he sought after the Lord, God caused him to succeed.*
> (2 Chronicles 26:5)

WHY FOLLOW GOD?

It seems the older I get, I grow less and less interested in running the "Rat Race." Young people attend schools of higher learning so they can attain that long strived for higher education. Some follow a passion, but most will tell you they attend college so they can make more money. Have you ever wondered why we do the things we do? What is the driving force that will make us go the extra mile, climb that hill, or simply do nothing?

Money and/or power are two of the most powerful motivating factors we will face. Some want the pretty girl or the handsome guy. I know a lot of people who have achieved some level of success but who now dream of having a job that isn't really a job but is a passion that can pay the bills.

When you ask someone in church why they follow God, you may get different answers depending on the church. Some have heard that when we follow God, we will be successful because God only wants good things for us. Others have heard that when we follow God, all of our problems magically disappear. Sadly, although those things would be nice, the Bible doesn't say any of that. But the Bible does say this: "For such people do not serve our Lord Jesus Christ, but their own appetites, and through smooth talk and flattery they deceive the hearts of the unsuspecting" (Romans 16:18).

So, why would someone follow God? We all have different needs at different times, but the reason I follow God is simple: because I choose to. Do I have problems? Sure, as does everyone, but God helps me through them. Am I rich? No, but I am content. I am also blessed beyond my wildest dreams with family, friends, and the assurance that I will, one day in my future, live forever in a mansion in a kingdom. I follow God because He leads me away from temptation and when I do fall, He helps me to my feet and tells me we are in this together.

God made the person who would eventually become me. He loves me beyond my ability to comprehend. He cares for me. He sent His only Son to die for me. He guides my steps and gives me light in the darkness.

Earthly riches are nice, but they cannot compare with heavenly treasures. And when we leave here, someone else comes along and picks them up. That's okay. While someone is spending whatever I leave behind, I will be basking in the glory that is an eternity with the One who made those treasures.

Eternal Father. Thank You for this earth and the life that I have. Thank You for my family and my friends. Thank You for the pets that have enriched my life. But mostly, thank You for the promise of the life I will one day have with You in Your heavenly kingdom. Amen.

> He said to them, "Go into all the world, and preach the gospel to every creature." (Mark 16:15)

BEING CONTAGIOUS

In our modern society, some people are scared to death. From Howard Hughes to A.J. (a producer for a local radio talk show) to someone you may know from work, or perhaps, you, our country is filled with people who are never without a bottle of hand sanitizer or some other cleaning product. And with the news of the day featuring stories of some new virus that, according to some, could be the next "Black Death" resurrected from the Middle Ages, a bit of extra caution is probably warranted. We use so many cleaning products that a whole industry has grown "filthy" rich due to our fear of germs and viruses and bacteria.

Let's face it, no one, including me, really likes being sick. The handshake has been replaced by the fist bump, the elbow touch, or the head nod. In some countries, the latest fashion accessory isn't jewelry or shoes, it's a color-coordinated facemask intended to filter out microscopic deadlies. Modern science has a name for this condition – germophobia – and the most extreme of these people are known as germaphobes. Germophobia: an irrational fear of germs and anything associated with them. Of all the phobias out there, I guess you could do worse.

Each year, we spend billions of dollars on things that are supposed to kill the things that are out to kill us. Soaps, antiseptics, and sanitizers – to name a few – can be found on nearly every kitchen or bathroom countertop. Yet, often despite our best efforts, the flu bug, the common cold, or some other malady will eventually bite most of us. We mention that we don't feel good, and we hear the inevitable reply, "Well, I hear it's going around." We say we catch whatever it is, but that's not true; it's the bug that catches us. The minute we let our guard down, we begin to feel bad and before we know it, bam!

What about us? Would any of us be found guilty of spreading God's word? As a Christian, could I honestly say that I am contagious? Am I actively trying to infect everybody I meet with what I have? If my

Christianity were a virus, would it be catchable? Would it be dangerous or perhaps life changing? Would I cause a spiritual pandemic or would I be just another short-lived inconvenience identified by a couple of sneezes, a cough or two, and then, gone before I was even noticed?

Christ didn't ask us to spread the gospel *if* we had the chance. You'll never find it in the Bible where Jesus said we should talk to others about salvation *unless* we have something better to do. Our charge is to be infectious. As Christians, we are carriers of the only thing that can change the world for the better. The world is sick with sin. We must tell the world about the cure. It is our job to catch somebody.

Lord Jesus. I pray You would give me the strength, courage, and conviction I need to go out and infect the world with Your good news. Amen.

This is eternal life: that they may know You, the only true God, and Jesus Christ, whom You have sent. (John 17:3)

KNOWING ABOUT GOD

I work for a large company with several thousand other employees who work in various locations throughout Alabama. When I'm working away from my office and someone finds out the name of my employer, I will sometimes be asked, "Do you know [enter name here]?" Because I have worked for this company for nearly 40 years, some I will know. But most of the time, my answer is either "No" or, "I know the name."

If you are asked to tell someone what you know about George Washington or Abraham Lincoln, your description will be based on what you were taught in history or perhaps something you may have read. If asked what I know about Amelia Earhart, I will respond that she was a famous pilot who died somewhere in the Pacific Ocean when she was trying to fly around the world. How about someone from modern times? How about Todd Beamer? You may not remember the person, but you will probably remember the event: Flight 93, September 11, 2001, Shanksville, Pennsylvania.

Let's try these, Barack Obama and Donald Trump. Both were elected President of the United States. Both are very famous. You probably know something about each of them. You may be able to name their wives and children. You may know what their favorite meal is or, if you really know them, their shoe size. But, when all is said and done, do you really know them?

Suppose you were asked the question, "Do you know God?" How would you answer? If your knowledge stops at believing that God is real and that He lives in heaven, you need to dig deeper. If you have read about Him in the Bible, that's a great start, but it's not good enough. Knowing God's attributes is like knowing the address of a bakery; you suspect the food is good, but you'll never know unless you taste it.

Reading the Bible and other study books about God are both good things. Listening to songs about God and Bible-based sermons will help you learn about God. All those are great but, in the end, if you and God aren't on a first name basis, if you don't have that personal relationship with Him, all of your knowledge will be for naught.

I would recognize Nick Saban or Kevin VanDam if I were to bump into them, but they wouldn't know me. On the rare occasion that I greet the president of the company I work for, I can call him by name, but I don't really know him, and I have no expectation that he knows anything about me. But when I arrive at heaven's gate and I see Jesus, even though that will be the first time I've actually seen Him, I know that I will know Him. What's the most important thing about that meeting? I know that Jesus will know me.

Eternal Father. I thank You that You know each of Your children by name. Amen.

> *Therefore, submit yourselves to God. Resist the devil, and he will flee from you.* (James 4:7)

WHO, OR WHAT, IS "IT"?

"Tag! You're it!" When I was a child, the games my friends and I played didn't involve television, the Internet, pushing buttons, or wearing a device on our face to be transported to some virtual world. Our games required sticks, rocks with some calm water, imagination, running, hiding, and other physical activity. Another thing about those games is that they didn't require much explanation.

Sledding in our part of the country was jumping on an old cardboard box and sliding down a pine straw-covered hill. Riding trees involved pine trees that weren't too big or too little. Climb to the top, kick your feet out, hold on, and ride them down. It was all fun and games until a tree broke and someone wound up getting hurt. Two other games we played had something in common: Hide and Seek or Tag. Both of those games had somebody who was "It." After deciding who "It" was, it was off to the woods or wherever we would be playing.

Looking back, I now wonder why did we call the person doing the hunting or the chasing "It"? In modern life, when confronted by an unknown foe, we tend to say, "It's after me." But why do we name it (whatever it is) "It"?

Deep down, we all fear the unknown. Somewhere out there, each of us has an unidentified foe that hides in the shadows, or maybe, we have something that is out to get us. We don't know who or what that person or thing is, so we name it the innocuous "It."

For the Christian, our "It" has a name, or rather, multiple names. The "It" that is out to get the Christian is called the devil, Satan, or Lucifer by many but he is known by other names: Prince of Darkness, Father of Lies, Accuser, Adversary, Angel of Light, the Antichrist, or Beelzebub, among others. One of the most descriptive names is found in First Peter, "Be sober and watchful, because your adversary the devil walks around as a roaring lion, seeking whom he may devour" (1 Peter 5:8).

Satan hides in our shadows, waiting for an opportunity to strike when we least expect him. If we stumble in our Christian walk, his goal is to keep us down, not to help us to our feet. Following modern trends, he will pull out a recording device and create a record of our failure for all to see.

"It" is a fine name for something unknown. Kids can still have their "It" when they play their games. But the eternal enemy of all things Christian is not unknown and he is not someone to play games with. When he jumps from his shadow, turn to him, call him by his name, and demand, in Jesus' name, that he leave!

My Savior, Jesus. I pray You would reveal to me the things of Satan so I could avoid his traps and deceptions in my daily walk. Amen.

> *Then I saw another angel flying in the midst of heaven, having the eternal gospel to preach to those who dwell on the earth, to every nation and tribe and tongue and people.*
> (Revelation 14:6)

FULL OF GOOD NEWS

Back in the "good old days," our ability to communicate was somewhat limited, when compared to today's technology. Years ago, if someone wanted to send a letter "across the pond," it had to travel weeks by ship. That same letter, if sent from New York to San Francisco, would typically be carried by a brave young lad riding a fast pony. Smoke signals were elementary communication but, throw in some wind or darkness, and those were fairly ineffective. Years passed and the telegraph made communication faster but not direct. Add a few years more and you find the telephone (for some of us, party lines meant you had to share your talk time) in most homes. In the event of an emergency, you might dial 0 to reach an operator or dial the number that your mother had taped to the wall beside the phone (because it was attached to that same wall). The modern emergency number, 911, was years from being commonplace.

Let's say you had some good news you wanted to share. If you received a new job, you either found a pay phone or you asked if there was a phone you could borrow. If the person you were trying to reach wasn't near a phone, your good news would have to wait. In other words, you were full of good news, but you couldn't tell anyone.

Fast-forward to today. You receive good news, and you pull out your cell phone and call whomever you want to tell. Better yet, if you really want to proclaim your news to any and all, with a few clicks on that same cell phone, practically the entire planet can be told. What was once only dreamed of can now be shouted from digital rooftops, should we choose to do so. So, tell me, if good news is so easy to tell, why does it seem so hard to spread the best news of all?

As Christians, we are literally filled to the brim with Good News. God has sent His Holy Spirit to live within us, ready to help us spread the Good News of the Gospel of Jesus Christ. We seem to have forgotten that, "a good report makes the bones healthy" (Proverbs 15:30b) and, "As cold waters to a thirsty soul, so is good news from a far country" (Proverbs 25:25). In a world thirsting for good news, the Good News of salvation that is available only from a relationship with Jesus Christ is the only water that can quench that thirst.

As Christians, we hold the knowledge of an eternity of peace, joyfulness, and rest. I'll admit, although we should, initially, we may not be comfortable sharing that news with everyone we see. But if we don't share it with everyone, can we at least share it with one?

Father God. Thank You for the Good News that is the salvation of Jesus Christ. On a daily basis, give us the courage, conviction, and strength to tell the ones You place in our path. Amen.

> *For the time will come when people will not endure sound doctrine, but they will gather to themselves teachers in accordance with their own desires, having itching ears, and they will turn their ears away from the truth and turn to myths.*
> (2 Timothy 4:3-4)

I'M TELLING YOU, SOMETHING'S NOT RIGHT

Depending on your point-of-view, a popular phrase that can be heard in today's politically charged climate is fake news. Fake, phony, fraud, counterfeit, pretend, false, untrue, misleading, or lies; no matter how we phrase it, we want the truth, the whole truth, and nothing but the truth, and we detest it when we get something other than the truth. Legal proceedings demand the truth, financial dealings require the truth, and relationships hinge on the truth. Our daily lives revolve around us knowing that certain things are true.

Have you ever received a counterfeit bill? Not a fake billing statement but a piece of paper currency that was not backed by the full faith and credit of the United States Treasury Department. I have seen some funny money that was obviously fake. The ink was the wrong color or the denomination was wrong (I don't know why we don't have $150.00 bills, but we don't). Things like that are easy for even a novice like me to spot. But one of the things a treasury agent must be able to spot is fake money.

A short time after being hired, a treasury agent is placed in a room with a table and on that table are bundles of real United States paper currency of various denominations and condition (i.e., some old bills, some new bills). Each day, that agent comes to work and each day that agent feels, smells, and looks at those bills. After a few days of looking at, smelling, and feeling real money, a few counterfeit bills of various quality are mixed in with the real thing. Experience shows that the agents who have been paying attention and applying their senses to their jobs are quick to point out the fake bills, regardless of the quality of the counterfeiter.

Our relationship with God is like that agent. The more time we spend with Him, praying, and reading His Word, we will find that we will become more familiar with the true God of the Bible. If we desire an authentic relationship with God, we must be willing to spend authentic time seeking out the real thing. Only after we spend time learning about God and what His Word teaches us will we be able to spot the difference between teaching that is true or false.

Speaking of money, how many times have you heard someone quote the famous scripture, "Money is the root of all evil?" You may have heard it from someone you looked up to as a person of religious authority. While that quote may indeed sound quite biblical, if you take a moment to read from First Timothy 6:10, you'll learn that the root of all evil isn't money. What the Bible actually says is that the *love* of money is the root of all evil. While this difference may seem minor, Revelation 22:18 cautions us to be accurate when we quote the words of the Bible.

I'm pretty sure I don't want to spend a lot of time learning how to spot a counterfeit fifty-dollar bill. What I do want to ensure is that I spend time with God and reading His Word so I will know the real thing when I see and hear it.

Father God. Let me see more and more of You as I read Your Word and spend time with You on a daily basis. Remind me not to let my doctrine be false nor my worship be counterfeit.
Amen.

We know that all things work together for good to those who love God, to those who are called according to His purpose.
(Romans 8:28)

WHY PICK JUDAS?

Nick Saban. Around Tuscaloosa, Alabama, the mere mention of those three syllables brings to mind an image of college football coaching royalty. As the head football coach of the University of Alabama, Coach Saban loses more assistant coaches to other schools each year than his team loses games. It seems that, other than when the next National Championship will come, Bama fans wonder how "Coach" will replace his most recent assistant coach departures.

For a second, imagine Coach Saban is interviewing candidates for a coaching vacancy. One of the coaches being considered has a history of being an outstanding position coach, but he isn't known as being the most loyal of coaches. He will hang in there with you until the times get rough, then he has a tendency to cut and run. He is also known as someone who does whatever he can to shift blame when something in his scheme doesn't work the way he thinks it should. Some would call him a "stirrer of the pot," not necessarily the best "team player." Do you think Coach Saban would hire him?

No one wants to pick someone they know will be a slacker. We all expect others to do what they can to make the team better. With that thought in mind, have you ever wondered why Jesus picked Judas Iscariot as one of His disciples, one of His inner-circle of followers? Because Jesus knows what we will do before even we know, He knew that Judas would one day betray Him to those who would hang Him from a cross. And yet, knowing all the while that Judas would be the one who knocked over one of the first dominos of what we now celebrate as the Easter season, Jesus chose Judas.

Although we don't understand why, Judas, and his future betrayal of Christ, was necessary for the fulfillment of God's plan. Could Judas, if he had asked for it, have been forgiven? God forgives all who are truly repentant of their sins, so I'm assuming He certainly would have forgiven Judas.

Thinking about that coach; I doubt Coach Saban would even grant him an interview. Head coaches need assistant coaches who are fully devoted to the team so the team will have the best chance of success.

If one of the other disciples had been able to talk to Jesus, do you think they would have said, "Jesus, can I talk to You about that Judas guy? Something about him just doesn't seem right." Jesus picked Judas because picking Judas was part of God's plan. After all, Jesus knew everything about me, and yet, He still chose to save me.

*Lord Jesus. I don't know why You would want someone like me to be on Your team, but I am thankful I'm asked to play a part. I pray I would be willing to participate when called by You.
Amen.*

Blessed are those who are persecuted for righteousness' sake, for theirs is the kingdom of heaven. (Matthew 5:10)

BANDWAGON JUMPERS

"Go Team!" "That's my team!" "We won!"

I know a lot of people who are fans of certain teams. In and around my hometown of Tuscaloosa, Alabama, there are a ton of people who are fans of the University of Alabama football team. While most of those fans are realistic, they understand that you can't win every game; some of those fans are, shall we say, extremely enthusiastic. That is, until . . .

Winning, and winning often, is fun. Celebrating a win is what every fan of every team wants and expects. Teams learn by winning. They learn what they did right. But most coaches will tell you real learning is done when you struggle a bit, or, heaven forbid, you lose. I have found, and sometimes I have been guilty of this same behavior, that behavior being when a team begins showing signs of trouble, the grumbling is never far behind.

First, you'll usually hear that you can't win every game. After a second loss, you will hear that the team has a little work to do. Three or more losses, the team is now in a rebuilding phase. But let a team go into a struggle of some lengthy duration – let's say four or five consecutive years – that's when you will find out which fans are true and which fans are not.

It's easy to become a fan of any particular team. Buy a t-shirt, wear a hat, watch a game or two, and, voila, you're a fan. Besides, if "your team" begins to struggle, there's always another team out there you can root for. There's a name for that kind of fan, Bandwagon Jumper.

Some seem to believe that being a Christian is kind of like that. Have a little faith, walk a little aisle, say a little prayer, take a little dip, and, voila, you're a Christian. And now that you're a Christian, you leave the church thinking that, because you've heard that you're on the winning team (yes, we do win, I know the ending to that story), from this point forward, life is going to be a breeze. If that's the only reason you joined this team, there's a little something you need to know:

Christianity doesn't work that way. Why do I say so? Because Jesus said so.

Second Timothy 3:12 tells me that all who desire to live for God will be persecuted. John 15:18 says I could be hated because the world hated Jesus. First John 3:13 goes on to tell me I shouldn't be surprised if the world hates me. Revelation 2:10 tells me to not fear what I will suffer. First Peter 4:12 says a fiery trial will test me. I could go on, but you probably get my – no, actually, Jesus' point. So why would anyone want to join a team that will only know suffering and pain? Is there any reward when you join Jesus' team?

Second Timothy 2:12 says that I will reign with Jesus if I endure. Romans 6:23 tells me that with Jesus, I will receive eternal life. James 1:12 says a crown of life waits for those who stand the test. First Corinthians 2:9 tells me that I cannot imagine what God has prepared for those who love Him. And Luke 6:23 plainly states that my reward in heaven is great. Again, I could go on, but to answer the question, yes, there may be persecution for those who become Christians, but there is a reward awaiting those who join God's team and endure until the end.

God wants all to be saved, but being saved doesn't guarantee that all your times will be good. Being on God's team will come with trials and persecutions. Christianity is not a "try it, see if you like it" type of commitment. If all you want is the hat, the t-shirt, and a few good times, you need to know this: Christianity is not a bandwagon you jump on based on the ease and enjoyment of life. But, if you want to join the team that wins in the end, this is the team for you.

Father God and Lord Jesus. Thank You for telling us the end of the story. I pray that those who are looking for the true winning team will find it in You. Amen.

> *Watch therefore, for you know neither the day nor the hour in which the Son of Man is coming.* (Matthew 25:13)

THE BOSS IS LOOKING

As I've said in other stories, I enjoy fishing. Naturally, I enjoy being on my boat casting a lure, but I also enjoy watching television programs about fishing. Anyone who enjoys a particular hobby is looking for ways to improve, and one can usually learn from those who make their living doing what we do for fun. Those who understand a little about modern fishing techniques know that electronics have really upped the game when it comes to locating fish, or at least the underwater features that fish tend to hang around. Building on that, a sponsor of outdoor television programs has an ad that features an electronic device of a totally different sort.

In the ad, a group of four professional fishermen have jobs in a corporate setting. Because the group prefers to be talking fishing or doing something related to fishing rather than working, they needed a way to know when the boss was near. Necessity being the mother of invention, one of the guys designed an electronic device that alerts the group when the boss is approaching. A beep sounds and a red-light flashes to alert the group that it's time to switch from fish talk to doing their "real" jobs. I know some people who would pay good money for such a device.

When it comes to work, I honestly don't know anyone who is 100% work 100% of the time. From time-to-time, we all need short breaks so we can re-focus on the task at hand and our employers, for the most part, understand that. The trouble comes when the boss begins to notice our diminished output because those breaks tend to get longer and more frequent. Eventually, the boss is forced to correct the situation, and we are forced to live with the consequences.

As someone nears the day of their retirement, they begin to look forward to that day when the alarm clock wakes them for something other than work. As a Christian, we look forward to one day going home to that promised house in the sky. Yes, we can plan our retirement date from our earthly job but none of us knows either the day we will leave this earth or the day Jesus will return to claim those who are His. While He walked this earth, Jesus gave many examples that we should be ready when that day finally comes.

No, there's no such thing as a boss detector. When my boss walks down the hall to my office, he's most likely going to find me doing whatever project I happen to be working on. Then again, he may walk into my office, close my door, take a seat, and we'll spend a few minutes talking about something other than work. Bosses need breaks, too. But when it comes to my Christian work, I want to make sure God finds me doing whatever He has asked me to do. Because God lives in my heart, I don't have to worry about Him sneaking up on me; He's always here.

Eternal Father. I thank You that You are always there with me. I know one day You will return to claim Your own. I pray when that day comes, if I am still here, You will find me doing that which You would have me do. Amen.

> *He who has an ear, let him hear what the Spirit says to the churches.* (Revelation 3:22)

HOW MANY TIMES?

"How many times do I have to tell you to [enter activity here]?" As a growing boy, I'm sure my mother thought those words twice as many times as she said them. And, yes, there were consequences to be paid for my not doing whatever it was that filled that blank. Let's see, there was clean my room, pick up my dirty clothes, cut the grass, do my homework, take a bath, brush my teeth; it was a long list. Momma (I still call her that) and every other parent or person in authority has moments when they feel they aren't being listened to by those who should be listening. I'm sure we've all had those moments when we want to gently place our hands on the shoulders of whomever is ignoring us and slowly say, "Look at me. Are you listening? I need you to focus on me. Right. Now."

As humans, some of us naturally seem to know how to do some things. Some people can pick up a camera, look through a viewfinder, and compose the perfect shot without so much as a whisper about the rule of thirds. Others can sit at a piano and play, having no idea of how to read music. There are those who look at a car's dead engine and have that thing purring like a kitten in just a few minutes. But each of those people have things with which they struggle. I've always been able to see the picture in the viewfinder, but I cannot make heads or tails of that thing known as advanced math.

For the Christian, if we would only live our lives based on the "Big Twelve" (the Ten Commandments plus what Jesus called the greatest commandments, "Love God" and "Love your neighbor as yourself"), how much closer would we be to what Christ taught when He walked throughout the Holy Land? But, as easy as those should be, we all have our struggles.

In the second and third chapters of Revelation, we read where Jesus told John to write letters to seven churches: Ephesus, Smyrna, Pergamum, Thyatira, Sardis, Philadelphia, and Laodicea. Each letter was unique for each church but each letter contained these fifteen words: "He who has an ear, let him hear what the Spirit says to the churches." While those letters were addressed to seven churches, that warning is meant for all churches and all Christians. We are to read each letter and apply it to our daily lives.

I know we sometimes want to say, "God, I know You probably get tired of forgiving me of my sins. But, since I'm talking to You, I need You to forgive [enter sin here]." You would think that we – at least I – would eventually learn.

I know that sometimes God probably wants to place His hands on my shoulders, look into my eyes and say, "Randy, look at Me. Are you listening? I need you to focus on me. Right. Now."

Father God. I know I don't deserve the forgiveness You freely give. I am so sorry I have to come to You time and again telling You how sorry I am because I have once again disappointed You. I am forever grateful that You love me enough to forgive me and if You have to place Your hands on my shoulders to guide me, let me feel those hands and follow their lead. Amen.

Then she said to the king, "True was the report that I heard in my land concerning your words and wisdom. But I did not believe their reports until I came and my eyes saw; and indeed, half the greatness of your wisdom was not declared to me. You have exceeded the report that I heard." (2 Chronicles 9:5-6)

THERE'S NO WAY

Years ago, the Museum of Art in Birmingham, Alabama, hosted a European Masters exhibit. I don't remember if I saw Mona Lisa, Starry Night, The Last Supper, or Storm on the Sea of Galilee. I do remember seeing plenty of paintings by some relatively well-known artists including Rembrandt, Van Gogh, Renoir, and Monet. While I am, by no means, a connoisseur of fine art – some makes me scratch my head and say, "I don't get it," – I do appreciate their talent. Many times, I would think to myself, "There's no way someone could paint that," and yet, there I stood looking at it. Fine art, as with other things, should be seen to be fully appreciated.

I am told you have to personally experience Times Square on New Year's Eve to understand the magnitude of the spectacle that is 1,000,000 people in a wad waiting for a ball to drop. I'll gladly take their word for it, but I'll pass. I have seen the Golden Gate Bridge and Niagara Falls, and both are unique in their own way. I've never been in a military conflict (a heartfelt thank you to all who have), I've never jumped from an airplane, and I've never broken free of the surly bonds of earth's gravity in a spaceship bound for the stars. Other places I've never seen would be the Grand Canyon, Yosemite, Ireland, Yellowstone, the African jungle, Australia; the list could go on. Maybe one day I will see these, but for now, I'll rely on the reports of others.

For the Christian, we are told that we do not possess the ability to imagine how beautiful is our promised heavenly home. "But as it is written, 'Eye has not seen, nor ear heard, nor has it entered into the heart of man the things which God has prepared for those who love Him'" (1 Corinthians 2:9). Heaven is that destination that we must experience to be believed, and I have a feeling that, if there is such a thing as awe in heaven, we will all stand and truly be in awe of the gift that is our heavenly home.

As for all those places I haven't seen, if my life ends without ever having experienced a single glimpse of any of them, I'll be okay. In the end, that really won't matter. But when I open my brand-new eyes in heaven and these lungs take their first heavenly breath, oh what a day that will be.

Eternal God and Heavenly Father. The more I think of the home You have for me in heaven, the more I cannot wait to see those pearly gates and to hear You welcome me home. Amen.

> *Since we have these promises, beloved, let us cleanse ourselves from all filthiness of the flesh and spirit, perfecting holiness in the fear of God.* (2 Corinthians 7:1)

PERISHABLE THINGS

Have you ever watched a top-tier athlete ply the tools of their trade? When we were young, my friends and I would pretend we were some NFL running back or NBA forward, doing our thing to imaginary crowds in our back yards. I enjoy NASCAR but I will never be able to drive a car like Kyle Busch or Dale Earnhardt. I enjoy fishing but Kevin Vandam can find fish where I would never think to cast a lure.

There was a time I played golf. I've never been great at it, but I have hit some pretty good shots and a few rounds left me feeling pretty good about my game. Any golfer who has watched the professionals play has thought, "If I had those clubs and had his coach, I could do that." Alas, for most of us hackers, the closest we will ever come to the ability of Tiger, Phil, Jack, Arnie, or Jordan (to name just a few) is to wear the same clothes, hit the same ball, and, once in a while, make that "un-makeable" putt.

Watching a professional golfer at the top of their game is – for a golfer – a thing of beauty. But even the best golfer doesn't win every round; they don't even win most rounds. And, for some unknown reason, the golfer who last month couldn't miss a fairway or a putt can't seem to do anything right this month. One thing about top athletes, they are always practicing to make their game better. Even that struggling golfer, to find themselves back at the top, must book some time with their coach, go to the range, and hit thousands of practice shots.

All skills are perishable. Sports, driving, typing, speaking, or singing, no matter what it is we do, if we neglect to practice, we, too, may find ourselves floundering, not quite at the top of our game. Being an effective Christian is the same. Once we surrender our lives – through faith – to the power and dominion of Jesus, we will always be Christians. But to be an effective Christ follower, we must read our Bible daily. To grow comfortable in prayer, we must constantly pray. In fact, the Bible tells us we are to pray about everything.

We, as Christians, must aspire to be the best Christians we can be. And to be *that* Christian (yes, when it comes to following Christ, we do want to be *that* guy or gal), just like Tiger Woods must hit the putting green if he wants the trophy, we must practice our spiritual skills in order to finish our spiritual race.

Father God. I pray I will continue to grow in my faith of You. Continue to point out the things I need to encourage, and those things I need to eliminate, to help that growth. Amen.

> *Woe to you, scribes and Pharisees, hypocrites! You cleanse the outside of the cup and dish, but inside they are full of extortion and greed. You blind Pharisee, first cleanse the inside of the cup and dish, that the outside of them may also be clean.*
> (Matthew 23:25-26)

WASHING DISHES

Every morning, at least on work mornings, I typically have two cups of coffee. I sip on one cup as I read God's Word and enjoy the other as I drive to work. The driving cup is one of the 20-ounce, stainless steel, double-insulated cups that has become popular because of its ability to keep hot things hot and cold things cold. My other cup, the reading cup, is a 12-ounce ceramic mug that was given to me many years ago. I have other cups that hold the same amount of coffee but this particular cup is my favorite. One, because it was a gift and, two, it perfectly fits my hand. I wash that cup each day because I know that tomorrow morning, I'm going to drink coffee from that cup.

No one wants to eat from a dirty dish or drink from a dirty cup. Have you ever sat down at a restaurant and noticed that the silverware isn't clean or the bottom of the plate has food from a previous diner? Some of you may accuse me of being picky, but I'm not going to use a fork or spoon that has remnants of a previous patron's food. I didn't then and I won't now.

Jesus cautions us against focusing all our attention on our external appearances, actions, and words, while our internal life – the thoughts and desires of our minds and hearts – are filled with greed, malice, spite, and ill-will. While we may see and hear the external works and words, God sees that which others cannot; He sees our thoughts, hopes, and desires. "But the Lord said to Samuel, 'Do not look on his appearance or on the height of his stature, because I have rejected him. For the Lord sees not as man sees. For man looks on the outward appearance, but the Lord looks on the heart'" (1 Samuel 16:7).

Clean clothes, good hygiene, and a large vocabulary may be nice goals, but having a clean heart and godly thoughts are the ultimate goal of the Christian. Just as we will not eat from a dirty dish or drink from an unclean cup, God insists we purge sinful things like pride, greed, covetousness, and judgment from our heart.

As much as I like my cup, I want it to be clean. I must wash both the outside and the inside. And as much as I want a clean cup, God wants a clean heart. If I won't overlook an unclean cup, why should I expect God to overlook my unclean thoughts?

Father God. Forgive me of my unclean thoughts and sinful desires. Continue to guide me in my steps, words, and thoughts. Show me the way so I may walk in it. Amen.

> *Then Jesus said to him, "Unless you see signs and wonders, you will not believe."* (John 4:48)

BELIEF IN A SIGN

If you travel far enough southwest on I-59/20 from Tuscaloosa, Alabama, you will eventually see a sign placed by the State of Mississippi welcoming you to The Magnolia State. Likewise, if you drive in an easterly direction from Mobile, a similar, yet different sign will welcome you to Florida, The Sunshine State. If you were to take the time to compare the soils from opposite sides of those signs, you would not know the difference between Mississippi dirt and Alabama dirt or dirt from Florida and dirt from Alabama. Since the land looks the same from state to state, the only way you know you've crossed from one to the other, in most cases, is because some sign said you did. If we're honest, the only way we believe we have crossed into another state is because some road crew installed a sign.

Let's suppose someone on that road crew was a little off when they staked the location of the sign, not far, let's say about one-hundred feet. Would you know the difference? When I fly in an airplane, I like to sit beside the window so I can watch the world streak by far beneath my feet. I often look at the land below, trying to guess where I am. But, unless I have a map or see some major landmark, I'm not able to tell when I cross from North Carolina to South Carolina or, for that matter, from the United States to Canada.

Let's face it; most of us believe things to be true because someone in alleged authority said it. While millions of people will believe a road sign is the gospel truth, many of those, for some reason, refuse to believe the truth of the Gospel. Some of the same people who believe a bright dot in the night's sky is Venus will, for some reason, not accept the fact that that dot was created by the same God who created them.

There are people who have no trouble accepting Einstein's theory of relativity as an ironclad truth, but they are not willing to admit that it is possible to spend an eternity with God, or, for that matter, apart from Him. The Bible plainly states that each of us has a place we will spend eternity. We are told how we can ensure our eternal future with God. One day in our future, we will pass from this life to the next and, although I haven't seen either of the two final destinations, I am beyond sure that I won't need a sign to tell me the difference between the two.

If you are willing to believe you are where you are because some sign tells you so, you should trust the map in the Bible that tells you how to get to that heavenly mansion with your name on it.

Father God. Thank You for the promise that Your Word is true. Thank You for the signs You put in our daily walk that tell us where we are and the path You want us to take. Amen.

> *I wait for the Lord, with bated breath I wait; I long for His Word! My soul waits for the Lord, more than watchmen for the morning, more than watchmen for the morning.*
> (Psalm 130:5-6)

LOOKING FORWARD TO IT

Sunny and Gracie. Anyone who knows me or has read some of my stories might recognize those two names. If not, allow me to introduce you to my two little girl dogs, Sunny, a terrier mix, and Gracie, a Chihuahua, both of them rescues. Sunny and Gracie love to hear the opening of my overhead garage door. As soon as I open the door that connects the garage to the kitchen, I find both of them just beyond the door, tails wagging, Gracie doing her little front feet dance, Sunny standing on her hind feet. I am greeted with all of this activity simply because I've returned home. No matter how long I've been outside, whether a couple of minutes to take out the garbage or to check the mail or if I'm returning home from a full day at work or fishing, they are thrilled that I have returned.

After giving them a snack, I'll head for my bedroom to take off my shoes and change clothes. As soon as I sit on the stool, Sunny jumps on my thighs, doing what she can to give my face a lick or two. Her tail wagging, she looks in my face and, if she could talk, I imagine she would tell me all about her day of guarding the house from boogers and bandits and whatever else threatened our castle. Gracie waits in the den for her turn. I'll grab a bottle of water, sit on the recliner, and, before I can extend the leg rest, she's in my lap, filling me in on her busy day. I can imagine her saying, "Where have you been? It's been practically FOREVER since you left. I thought you were never coming back." I will admit, seeing them so happy just because I'm me and I'm home brings a smile to my face.

Are we like that with God? When we finish reading His Word and mark our place, do we look forward to the next time we can turn those pages? Do we yearn to hear His still voice or feel His gentle touch as He guides us through this life He has given us? Do we ever sit down and think about heaven as we read the 21st chapter of Revelation? Do you wonder if there will really be streets made of pure gold? How I look forward to a time of no tears, sadness, grief, or pain. And when I am shown my new house (or room or mansion) by the One who promised I would have one, what a glorious day that will be. Right now, as I sit here and think about it, man, if I had a tail, would it be wagging.

Sadly, some are so busy with the cares of this life, they don't make time to think about the life to come or to even acknowledge God's presence. When it comes to seeing God, I choose to be like Sunny and Gracie. I choose to dance, to be joyful, and to twirl around with glee. Maybe, just maybe, I can bring a smile to His face.

Lord Jesus. I know to some You have been gone so long it seems You are never coming back. Let us remember our time is not Your time and You don't go by our calendar. Let me continue to look forward to Your return with the same joy that Sunny and Gracie have for me. Amen.

> *He who believes in Him is not condemned. But he who does not believe is condemned already, because he has not believed in the name of the only begotten Son of God.* (John 3:18)

SALVATION IS NOT...

When I was a mere child, how many times did I hear the phrase, "Back in the good old days"? Another phrase that I heard a lot and now use, since I'm entering my seventh decade of life is this: "Back when I was a kid . . ." In these days of a virtually unlimited number of electronic games, back when I was a kid, in the good old days, we either played outside, put together jigsaw puzzles, or played board games. On those days when it was going to be too nasty to go outside (which had to be very nasty, indeed), we would pull out the game, *Monopoly*.

If you've never played *Monopoly*, believe me, it takes a *very long time* to determine a winner. If you wanted, and if everyone agreed, you could change the rules to make for a speedier game, but we often played by the rules of the game. As you played, you would find yourself buying properties and collecting either Chance cards or Community Chest cards. One card you wanted in your pile of stuff was a "Get Out Of Jail Free" card. Inevitably, as the game was played, you would land on THAT square (if you've played, you know WHICH square) and you would have to "Go Directly To Jail – Do Not Pass Go – Do Not Collect $200." If you had THE card, you would go to jail and flash THE card, allowing you to simply visit jail and continue your way to board game domination. The one thing having that card did not allow was to play the game as if the rules didn't apply.

I've heard it said by some that salvation is the spiritual equivalent of a "Get Out Of Hell Free" card. Those who look at salvation like that often live life as if God's rules don't apply to their life. Just because we read that people who believe in God's Son are not judged guilty does not remove the responsibility of living by God's rules. In reality, after we receive salvation, it becomes more important that we learn and obey the will of God in our daily words, actions, and, yes, according to Matthew 9:4, even our thoughts. We may think that our actions belong to us and, if we think that, we are thinking wrong. Romans 14:20-21 tells me that if I do things that cause others to sin, then I am doing the wrong things.

Even those Monopoly players who have the "Get Out Of Jail Free" card must first go to jail to use it. As a Christian, I am promised I will never go to the eternal jail that is hell. Salvation is not a card to be flashed before you sin just because you want to sin. Salvation is a gift to be treasured above all other gifts. Yes, you could lose the game of *Monopoly* if you can't get out of jail free, but not having salvation when you leave this earth will cost you more than any game.

You're right, your salvation card is free, but the cost of not having it, at the end of this game we call life, is anything but.

Christ Jesus, remind me to never take Your gift of eternal salvation for granted or to play it like some trivial trinket. I know that, while my salvation cost me nothing, the cost You paid to obtain my salvation was everything. Amen.

See then that you walk carefully, not as fools, but as wise men, making the most of the time because the days are evil.
(Ephesians 5:15-16)

WATCH YOUR STEP

I've done a lot of walking in my life; a vast majority of it was done on smooth, level surfaces, but not all. Whether we do our walking through carpeted hallways, on the hardwood floor of the executive suite, on the slickest rocks in the Cahaba River, or through the forest of a National Park, each of us is far better served when we watch where we place each step.

By not watching where we are going, we may step in a mudhole or on a snake, we could suffer injury should we slip on that river rock and turn an ankle, or we may even walk right off the edge of a cliff. When we add unfamiliarity, inclement weather, or darkness, the odds of missing a step increase to the point that the likelihood of an incident is greatly increased.

Let's face it; we all walk better when we know where we are going and when we stay on the defined path. Some will say we miss so much of the world by not venturing from the established path but, when it comes to our Christian walk, we are far better served when we stay on the path that God has chosen for us. This life can be an endless maze of the potholes of temptation, the loose gravel of the Internet, the times we slide back down the hill that we had struggled so hard to climb, and other opportunities for us to yield to Satan's temptations.

You don't have to look too far into the Bible to find out that God has planned out the steps we should take throughout our life. "A man's heart devises his way, but the Lord directs his steps" (Proverbs 16:9). "The steps of a man are made firm by the Lord; He delights in his way" (Psalm 37:23). "O Lord, I know that the way of man is not in himself; it is not in man who walks to direct his steps" (Jeremiah 10:23).

When we are planning a vacation, we draw out a map that includes the things we want to see and the places we will stop to rest or eat. Before we were born, God planned our life so we can avoid the pitfalls

Satan has laid out for us. "Your eyes saw me unformed, yet in Your book all my days were written, before any of them came into being" (Psalm 139:16). When we realize that our path is laid out by the God that created everything, we will find the walking easier, and we won't have to clean our shoes nearly as often.

Eternal Father. The next time I am tempted to go my own way, remind me that You have planned out my life even down to the steps I should take. Amen.

Now He who supplies seed to the sower and supplies bread for your food will also multiply your seed sown and increase the fruits of your righteousness. So you will be enriched in everything to all bountifulness, which makes us give thanks to God. (2 Corinthians 9:10-11)

THINGS THAT LAST

Although I don't travel much these days, I used to spend a good deal of time near the Alabama coastline in the towns of Gulf Shores and Orange Beach. I would fly kites, fish, eat seafood, and walk along the shore. If you've ever walked along the beach, you might turn to see your perfectly formed footprints in the sand, just beyond the reach of the constant salt-water waves. After walking for a while, I would turn and begin walking back to my starting point. On the way back, I always noticed that, while some of my footprints were still as I had made them, most of them were either partially or completely washed away, as if they had never existed. And if I returned the following morning, none of my footprints would be found. Those prints, although they had been made just a few hours earlier, now only survived in my memory.

Some people will be remembered because of some invention they had a part in creating. The memory of others will live on because of some words they had written, a speech they may have given, or a song they may have sung. I don't have to say much more than, "It was the best of times, it was the worst of times," or "It is a dream that is deeply rooted in the American dream," or "And the home of the brave," for most of us to think of Charles Dickens, Martin Luther King, Jr., or Francis Scott Key. Although many of us will never be as famous as those men, most of us will leave memories that will survive with our families and friends.

The Bible tells us to plant seeds as we go through life. Although a farmer plants seeds that will feed people throughout the world, he will most likely not meet the people whose lives his seeds impacted nor will he know the positive difference made by those seeds. There's a good chance the piece of salmon you enjoy for dinner was caught, maybe in

Alaska, by someone you will never meet. The apple we eat came from a tree that was planted from a seed that came from an apple that . . . I'm sure you get the point. We may never see the harvest, but we are told to plant the seeds.

Our introduction to the Gospel of salvation didn't begin with the person who told us; the world was introduced to that Gospel on a hill outside Jerusalem nearly 2,000 years ago. Jesus planted the seed of our salvation on that hill when He gave His life so we could live, not during this day or this year, but throughout eternity when we arrive at our heavenly home.

A farmer plants seeds in an effort to ensure there are crops available to feed those in need. If we follow what God tells us to do, we should make sure the seeds we plant are those of eternity. It is our job to plant the seeds of things that last.

Eternal God, thank You for the seed of salvation Your Son planted when He gave His life for us on that hill so many years ago. I thank You for the ones who made sure I would hear about that free gift when I was young. And I pray that I will continue planting the seeds You would have me plant. Amen.

> *I have blotted out, as a thick cloud, your transgressions, and your sins, as a cloud. Return to Me, for I have redeemed you.*
> (Isaiah 44:22)

MY DELETE KEY

I do a lot of typing, whether at work, on my home computer, or my phone. A lot of my job involves writing reports, developing or updating training programs or manuals, and composing or replying to emails. Home typing involves creative writing (such as the sentence you just read). "Typing" on my phone (if you call using two thumbs or one finger typing) is a lot of texting, emailing, Internet searching, and other general stuff. So, if you were to ask how many times I touch a keyboard in a typical day, my answer would be somewhere north of 50,000.

At home, I've used the same Apple computer for more than 10 years. In computer years, this machine is ancient. The wireless keyboard has seen many a battery change, but it still does everything I need it to do. Things at work are different; there we get a new machine every three years. Since I've been at my present job, I've gone through three computers and I'm nearing another replacement. The last two times the IT guy has swapped my unit, I made sure that he took the new keyboard with the old computer.

While some don't care about a keyboard, I do. Although we have Dell computers at work and I'm fine with Dell computers, I don't like Dell keyboards. After a bit of trial and error, I finally found one that sits at the correct angle, has the right touch of the keys, and a comfortable mouse. You can tell that keyboard has been used a lot because a few of the letters are nearly missing. If you were to look at the keyboard and guess which keys I use the most, you will probably say A, E, S, G, T, and H. Sure, I use those, but they aren't the ones I use the most.

The two keys I use the most are not alpha nor are they number keys. Those two keys would be Delete and Backspace. Why those two keys? Those two are my "fix it" keys. I need "fix it" keys because when I type, I make mistakes. Some days, I make a lot of mistakes. And yes, there are days I make so many mistakes that I'm tempted to delete the entire document and start over.

Wouldn't life be great if we could just press Delete or Backspace when we say or do something we know we shouldn't? If the screen of our lives was visible and the words we were about to say would appear on that screen BEFORE we said them, how many times would we press the Delete or the Backspace key? Now that I think of it, having that set up would make life a lot better. I know in my case if I had a Delete key, I could pretty much eliminate the need for that "I'm sorry" button I've had to press too many times.

No, we don't have a Delete key to remove our sins, but we do have God. We can't magically erase the sin from our life, but we can ask God to take it away. The best thing about God removing our sin is that He never remembers them. "For I will forgive their iniquity, and I will remember their sin no more" (Jeremiah 31:34c). I'm not sure about you, but I like the idea of a God that can do that.

Father God. I thank You for the forgiveness of the sins You have deleted from my life. And I thank You for never remembering them again. Amen.

> Jesus said to him, "I am the way, the truth, and the life. No one comes to the Father except through Me." (John 14:6)

ONE GATE

I work for a large company that employs roughly 6,500 people at facilities and offices scattered throughout Alabama. The location where I work has multiple buildings and training areas on nearly 425 acres of land. The warehouses, repair shops, garages, and statewide training facility are collectively known as "The Complex." Typically, I travel one route to get to work and to return home, but depending on traffic or road conditions, there are two or three other routes I may use.

Of all the routes that I and the 400 other people that work at this site travel, access to our facility is typically available via a single gate. When we arrive at work, the gate will not open until a scanner reads our I.D. badge that has an embedded digital chip. On-site security must be told in advance if we are expecting a visitor to our site, or the visitor will have to wait until someone can come to the gate to escort them on the property. I sometimes wonder if we have gone slightly overboard, but those are the rules and to work there, I must comply with the rules.

Heaven is much like our worksite. There are many ways someone can learn about getting into heaven. The Bible and other books, teachers, pastors, the Internet, television, radio, and others who know and are willing to share the path to heaven are all resources for learning the key to heavenly entrance. Even though there are multiple ways to learn about heavenly access, there is but a single gate through which you must walk.

That one gate – forgiveness of our sin through the blood of Jesus – is the only gate that allows entrance into eternal paradise. You must have your name written in the reservation book. The blood that Jesus shed as He hung on the cross, a willing sacrifice to atone for our sins, is the ink that writes your name. Unlike the gate at my workplace, if you arrive at heaven's gate without having your name written in the book of eternal life, no one, not even Jesus, will come to the gate and escort you in. You, and you alone, must have made your reservation before you take the trip.

Yes, sometimes the rules we have to follow are aggravating, but rules are a necessary part of life. Getting into heaven doesn't require a secret password, some mystical handshake, or a swipe of a computerized badge. God made heavenly entrance simple and straightforward: repent of your sins and ask for and receive salvation. There is no other way.

Heavenly Savior. Words cannot express how I look forward to the day when I arrive at heaven's single gate and hear the words, "Randy, you're here. Come on in." Amen.

When the devil had ended all the temptations, he departed from Him until another time. (Luke 4:13)

UNTIL NEXT TIME

Next time. The eternal hope of the one who loses a contest. Watch a sporting contest and you may hear the loser utter the challenge, "Two out of three?" Someone loses a bet and they will ask the victor, "Double or nothing?" Whenever all great – or even not-so-great – rivals have a contest, the one who comes out on the short end of the score walks away, promising that the next time will be different.

Almost everyone who follows competitive sports has heard the phrase, "Second place is first loser." Moral victories may be nice, but the lessons of 100 moral victories will never fill a trophy case. Competitors compete for one reason: to win. In any sport, the greater the competitor, the greater the desire to win. Competitors want the big trophy, the blue ribbon, the gold medal, the blanket of roses, or the highest step on the podium. To the victor go the spoils, the ticker-tape parades, and the White House visits. Sure, the one who finishes in second place will tell you that a lot can be learned from finishing in second place. The thing they won't tell you is that the lesson they most learned is that second place is not first. On the outside, the fiercest competitor will smile and shake the hand of the winner, but, on the inside, they are screaming, "Next Time!"

When it comes to spiritual competition, Satan, a competitor who, in his mind, has no equal, has lived ten thousand lifetimes of "next time." When he was kicked out of heaven (because he wanted to be first among all), as he fell from his used-to-be home, I can imagine him pointing his now defeated finger at God and screaming, "I'll get you next time!" His first "next time" was in the Garden of Eden. Not long after he had convinced Eve to disobey God, he won a second victory when Adam also disobeyed. Sometime later, he quickly claimed a "next time" victory in the field when Cain, filled with jealousy because God favored Abel's offering, murdered his brother. God had to flood the earth because of Satan and his quest for "next time." Sodom and

Gomorrah were two more of Satan's "next times" as was David seeing Bathsheba take a bath.

Satan saw an opportunity for his greatest "next time" as he watched Jesus roam in the wilderness. If he could only get Jesus to obey him rather than God, Satan knew he would have the ultimate "next time." But, as hard as he tried, that "next time" never happened. Jesus, though tired, hungry, and physically weakened, would not yield to Satan and his bag of tricks. As many victories as Satan had celebrated over humanity, Jesus was the one victory he could not, nor would not ever, claim. Satan thought he had won at Golgotha but, a mere couple of days later, when Jesus emerged from the tomb meant for the dead, He would claim ultimate victory over Satan and his endless quest to best God.

Just because Satan lost that battle, don't think he gave up. In Acts 5:3, after Jesus had ascended from earth to heaven, Peter asked Ananias why Satan had filled his heart causing him to lie to the Holy Spirit. As simple as it sounds, the answer is "next time."

Even today, Satan sees each of us as his personal "next time" competition. When we are tempted, we need to recognize it for what it is and pray to God for strength so we don't become another notch in Satan's belt. Face your enemy and strongly proclaim, "No Satan, not this time."

Lord of heaven and earth, I know that Satan has me and all of Your creation on his list of targets. Give me the strength, courage, and conviction to tell him that I am Yours for all time. Because I am Yours, let me never be a reason for Satan to celebrate "next time." Amen.

> *For all that do these things are an abomination to the Lord, and because of these abominations the Lord Your God will drive them out from before you.* (Deuteronomy 18:12)

JUST ONE THING

We all have habits. We all have things that we have done or said so many times they have become second nature, so much that we do or say them without so much as a second thought. Habits can be good or bad and most of us have one or two of each. If we are honest, we are our habits, and our habits are us. But are our habits what they should be?

Looking at the habits that had entrenched themselves into my daily routine, I made a mental list of those things that I typically did that took me closer to God. In a second column, I identified the things that took my attention away from God. I made a promise to myself that I would begin to eliminate from my life those things listed in the second column. Some things were easy but others, not so much. I needed help to eliminate those things. I turned them over to God.

Do you have something, at least one thing, you can eliminate from your life so you can give that time to God? From experience, the eliminating something is the easy part; it's giving that time to God that has proven to be the hard part. It seems the minute you eliminate something, one or two other things are standing there, ready to take the place of that which you have just marked off. Why do we need to eliminate things? Because, if we let them, they will take the place of God.

In the Old Testament, God told Israel to wipe out certain groups of people because God knew the Israelites would intermingle with those groups. God knew if those people were allowed to co-exist with Israel, the Israelites would take on the customs and worship practices of the pagans and begin to worship other gods. God knew the only way to keep Israel's focus on Him was to remove the other things that would fight for that same focus. Did Israel wipe out all of the other peoples? No. Did Israel do what God knew they would and start worshiping the false gods? Sadly, some did.

Bad habits, now as well as those in ancient times, are easy traps that Satan sets for us. If we want to have a deeper relationship with God, we must rid our lives of those things that take our focus from Him. Do you have multiple things that do that? Pick out one and work on it. Pray to God to help you. But you must be willing to devote that newly found spare time to God.

When it comes down to it, something is either for God or it is not. Pick that which is good and eliminate that which is not.

Father God. Thank You for showing me the things that took my focus from You. I pray You will continue to point out those things so I can focus more and more on You. Amen.

The Lord is my shepherd, I shall not want.
(Psalm 23:1)

WANTING WHAT I HAVE

The shiny object. New and improved. As seen on TV. Black Friday Special Price Reduction – up to 150% OFF!!! Better than Black Friday Sale!!! But Wait!!! There's More!!! And if you buy within the next 10 minutes . . . It seems everywhere we look, especially in November or December, someone is trying to sell us something. I'll admit, I've fallen prey to the, "what I have works perfectly well but that one is NEW," shopping bug. I will stroll through a store and tell every salesperson I see that, "I'm just looking." Then I see it, that something I didn't know I wanted until it caught my eye.

I wear a perfectly functional work watch. This watch has done its job for more than 20 years. The band has been replaced five times and I don't know how many batteries have been changed, but it still works. The crystal is scratched and sweat has eaten away at the chrome on the back until mostly base metal is all that remains. I have considered replacing it with a watch that charges itself with the power of light. This new watch has a band that will last for years, possibly outliving me. Yet, each time I try it on, I hear a small voice in my ear asking me what's wrong with the watch I have? After a couple of minutes, I remove the watch from my wrist, telling the clerk thank you. "Maybe later," I tell myself.

Sometimes we see the blessings of others and we are tempted to ask God, "Why does he have that?" or "Why is their family perfect?" or "Why can't I sing like her?" It seems that God gives some things to others while denying them from us. No matter how hard I pray, why is it that my plan and God's plan for my life sometimes seem to be diametrically opposed? Then I read Proverbs 16:9 where I am told that I will plan, but God directs my steps. So much for plans.

We sometimes wonder why God seems to always have something for us to do in His service. We're fine with serving God, but do we ever wonder why He doesn't give old 'so-and-so' some of this service work?

If we listen for an answer, and we should because we did ask, we will probably hear what Jesus told Peter from the book of John. "When Peter saw him, he said to Jesus, 'Lord, what about this man?' Jesus said to him, 'If it is My will that he remain until I come, what is it to you? Follow Me!'" (John 21:21-22).

When we are honest, we will admit that God has plans for us, although we may not understand them. Isaiah 55:9 tells me that God's ways and thoughts are higher than mine. Philippians 4:19 promises that God will supply all my needs. We may convince ourselves that the new watch, the upgraded house, the work promotion, or the latest smartphone will be the last thing we will need, and it will – at least until the next new watch, house, promotion, or even smarter smartphone comes along. When we wonder why our plan doesn't match God's plan, we need to step back and remember that, so far, God's plan has worked pretty well.

Over the years, I've learned that most of my "mess-ups" happen when I want something that I don't have. It is then I need to want the bird I have in my hand instead of trying to catch the two that are in the bush. And last I checked, that old watch still gives the right time.

Lord, Thank You for the life You've given me. The next time I begin with my plans, tap me on the shoulder and ask me what time it is. I need to remember if that watch is good enough for You, it should be good enough for me. Amen.

> *He who believes in the Son has eternal life. He who does not believe the Son shall not see life, but the wrath of God remains on him.* (John 3:36)

PLAN B

"So. That didn't work. On to Plan B." How many times have I said or heard those words? To paraphrase Mike Tyson, at one time one of the most formidable men to enter a boxing ring, we all have a plan until reality punches us in the face. Spontaneity is no plan, nor is hope. Over my life, I've started and completed many projects, some of them complex and time-consuming, most simple and fairly straightforward. Many of these were completed as planned, but there were some that needed a Plan B or a Plan C or a Plan D.

Once, a young couple hired me to photograph their wedding. Two weeks before the wedding date, the bride-to-be called me, telling me that the Plan A facility they had booked had been foreclosed and left them without a venue. They had worked out a Plan B and were making sure I would be able to work with them. After learning the new wedding location, I agreed to the change.

The day of the now outdoor wedding arrived with sunshine and pleasant temperatures. The scene was very nice with a perfectly manicured lawn that sloped gently to a large lake. The pre-wedding photos of both the bride and groom went off without a hitch. As I sat in a chair, I noticed some dark clouds building in the southern sky. I checked a weather radar app on my phone and the colors converging on our location told me all I needed to know. I asked the wedding director if she had a Plan C. When she asked why, I showed her the radar and told her that Plan B was about to get wet and I didn't take photographs while standing in the rain.

She turned to a young man helping her and, with a decisiveness that many could learn from, she gave the following order: "Go up there and move those tractors out of the barn. We have forty-five minutes to get this stuff up there and have a wedding." Within an hour, the barn had been magically transformed into a makeshift wedding chapel. The wedding went off without any problems despite the walls having tools hanging on hooks and large raindrops falling just beyond the metal walls.

When it comes to life, we had better have a Plan B for pretty much any Plan A. The unexpected is always lying in wait and will seemingly strike at the most inopportune of times. But when it comes to eternity, there is no such thing as Plan B.

Yes, the Christian God is a God of second chances. He gives us ample opportunity to reserve entrance into our eternal heavenly home. We have the guidebook and we have many ways to learn how to be saved. He has sent a helper – the Holy Spirit – to assist us through life. But, when our earthly life is over, God is no longer a second chance God; He then becomes a Plan A God. Heaven has no Plan B. Look though you may, you won't find a "we'll try to work you in" policy anywhere in the Bible.

What was learned from the wedding? If anything, as we walk through this thing we call life, we had better have contingency plans. As far as I know, the couple who began their life as husband and wife in a barn during a thunderstorm is still happily married. If you are holding on to the idea that God will rearrange things because you didn't follow through with Plan A, let's just say there won't be any emergency plan for moving things out of that barn.

Eternal Father. Thank You for giving us everything we need to understand how we can spend eternity with You and Your Son in heaven. Thank You for our second chances, but thank You for Plan A. Amen.

> *There is no salvation in any other, for there is no other name under heaven given among men by which we must be saved.*
> (Acts 4:12)

NO APP FOR THAT

It finally happened. My affirmation from over forty years ago came back to bite me – kind of. I was measuring my boat trailer and needed to know the angle of a triangle. I remembered that the three angles of the triangle must equal 180 degrees. I knew one of the angles was 90 degrees. I knew the length of the three sides. What I didn't know was how to figure the other two angles.

I can hear some of you out there right now. You probably have your hand up and you are squiggling in your seat, telling me to use the Pythagorean Theorem. I know you are because a guy I know at work actually likes advanced math and he is just like you. "That's easy," he said when I told him what I needed, "all you have to do is use the Pythagorean Theorem." I just looked at him and shook my head.

Pythagorean. Yeah, that's one way; I *could* do that. Orrrrr. I *could* search my smartphone's digital application catalogue for an app. So I tapped that catalogue app and typed "Angle finder" in the search field. It just so happens that there are a lot of apps for that. One quick tap of the Buy button (exactly why do we call them buttons?) and after a few short seconds, I had my answers.

Our life is now filled with computer applications, or apps. Think of something you need and most likely, there's an app for that. Weather, lots of apps. Sports, are you kidding? The word processing software I am using as I tap this keyboard, is nothing more than a computer application. Travel plans, get the app first and you can save money and time. While some apps are pretty much worthless, most apps are actually helpful. But, there are some jobs that an app cannot do.

An app can't set a power pole. An app can't clean a fish. I don't use an app to wash, dry, or iron my clothes. On second thought, all three of those appliances – washer, dryer, and iron – have some sort of computer that helps control what they do. The more I think about it, there is an app for just about everything. Except . . .

The Bible tells me that there is no app that can save me from my sins. It wasn't a computer-generated hologram that died on that cross. No amount of gee-whiz digital magic was responsible for Jesus rising from the tomb. Acts 4:12 pretty well sums it up; only Jesus can save us from our sins. There may be apps that tell us the plan of salvation but only Jesus can follow through on that plan.

Do you need to know how to bake a cake, replace a broken doorknob, or make crystal-clear ice to impress your friends? Get an app. Do you want to be saved from your sins? There's no app for that. Oh yeah, what were those angles? 39.289° and 50.711°. You gotta love precision.

Lord God. I'm thankful we have things to help us get through our day. Most of all, I thank You for sending Your Son and for Your plan of eternal salvation. And yes, I'm thankful You created whoever it was who designed that app. Amen.

> *By this we know we are in Him. Whoever says he remains in Him ought to walk as He walked.* (1 John 2:5b-6)

EXACTLY LIKE ME

I don't have a brother. I have two sisters, both younger than me. I have twin grandchildren, a boy and a girl. When I told someone that I had twin grands, a boy and a girl, they asked me, "Are they identical?" I asked them if they listened to everyone as well as they listened to me. I work with a woman who has triplets, two girls and one boy. The girls look very much like one another, but their mother tells me each of them is their own person.

Several years ago, I was working in Mobile, Alabama. When I returned home one Friday, I was asked why I had been at Gorgas Steam Plant that week. I found that strange because Plant Gorgas and Mobile are separated by about 200 miles. After assuring the questioner that I had indeed been in Mobile all week, we decided that I must have a "twin brother" who is not related to me. In other words, I have a doppelganger.

According to dictionary.com, a doppelganger is an apparition or double of a living person. According to the people who saw this person, he was my height and weight, had the same hair color, sounded like me, and had the same eye color. He could have passed for my twin, and to some people, evidently, he did. Even though he looked, walked, and sounded like me, he wasn't me.

Around the world, we are told that every one of us has at least one, if not several, doppelgangers. Even if you have identical siblings, you and your sibling or your doppelganger are not exactly the same. While science tells us that we all have unique DNA, fingerprints, and iris patterns, we now know that the pattern of the veins in our hands is the most unique thing about us; no two people have the exact same vein pattern. Despite all that, we all have someone with whom we should want to be identical.

Every Christian, regardless of gender, race, age, or nationality should aspire to be just like Jesus. Jesus came to earth to show us how to live. Jesus told us that He was the human example of God, "He who has seen Me has seen the Father" (John 14:9b).

No, I never met my doppelganger. We've never stood side by side. I don't know his name or where he lives. But I do know Jesus. And while I'll never look like Jesus, my goal, as one of His followers, should be to live exactly like Him. As Christians, we should all strive to be the spiritual doppelganger of Jesus.

Jesus my Lord and Savior. Help me to live my life so others would see You in my walk and hear You in my words. May my life be a reflection of the life You would have me live. Amen.

> *But the fruit of the Spirit is love, joy, peace, patience, gentleness, goodness, faith, meekness, and self-control; against such there is no law.* (Galatians 5:22-23)

God's Fruit Basket

The fruit basket. The gift you send when you don't know what to give. Over the years, I've spent some time in hospital rooms and during many of those stays I would receive at least one fruit basket. Most of them included bananas, apples, oranges, grapes, and the occasional pear. Today, with the focus on healthy snacking, we have one or two baskets of fruit sitting in our lobby at work, encouraging us to make smarter nutritional choices. That's okay; I've got a stash of real snacks in one of my desk drawers when I don't feel like being particularly healthy. I know, I should eat the fruit.

Fruit is God's gift to the snack world. In addition to the long-established staples, kiwi, strawberries, pineapple, mango, melon, and dragon fruit (tasted it, not sure why people eat it) have found their way into our modern, between-meal snack regimens. I am told that fruit is a healthy alternative to the individually wrapped, processed sugar-loaded pastries that are so good or the flavored fried potato slices that dominate the snack aisles in any grocery store. While one serving of processed goodness isn't that bad, when we allow them to take over our lives, we are faced with nasties like growing waistlines and rising blood sugar levels.

Other than the fruits we eat, God gives us spiritual fruits. While the fruits we eat can quell our hunger pangs, fruits of the Spirit are intended to replenish our spiritual needs. When our soul is sad, God can send gentleness or joy our way. When we grow tired of waiting, God has a healthy dose of patience or self-control ready for us to take in. Love and peace are especially made for those who struggle with anger. Someone does us wrong and, instead of lashing out as Satan would have us do, we can return the slight with a heaping helping of kindness or goodness, and just for good measure, we can throw in a kind wave and a smile.

The fruit we have at work is free for the taking. We have no excuse for eating those processed snacks (but they're so good). When it comes to God's fruit basket, each morning we should load up with all we can carry. You just never know when you're gonna need some faithfulness or a touch of love to satisfy a pang of spiritual hunger.

Dear God. Just as I thank You for the food You give me when I am hungry, I thank You for the basket full of spiritual fruits that is mine for the taking. Amen.

Mary Magdalene came and told the disciples that she had seen the Lord and that He had said these things to her.
(John 20:18)

A DAY TO CELEBRATE

September 3, 1783. April 9, 1865. June 28, 1919. May 7, 1945. September 2, 1945. Do any of those dates ring a bell? If you are a student of American history, there's a good chance you know the significance of at least one or two. Throughout history, wars have been fought and, in most cases, wars came to an end. Some wars, like the legendary feud between the Hatfields and the McCoys in the Tug Valley region of West Virginia and Kentucky finally ended when both families grew tired of the fighting. Other wars, like those indicated by the dates above, ended with a formal ceremony in which representatives of the warring sides signed a treaty, signifying the end of hostilities.

At the end of every conflict, there is a victor and a surrendering party. In most cases, prisoners are returned and concessions are given and received. Hostilities are ended and, for a while, peace is realized, at least until the next shot is fired. Most major victories are marked by some sort of celebration, perhaps a national holiday or a parade. Of all the conflicts that ended in victory, no single victory changed history, as did the battle that began on a hill and ended at a small tomb outside the Israeli town of Jerusalem.

This war was fought not over land or riches but for the very soul of man. On that Sunday morning sometime between 27 and 33 A.D., Jesus claimed the ultimate victory. His opponent, Lucifer, Jesus' one-time ally, thought he had won as he watched Jesus die on the cross. Satan, as Lucifer is also known, celebrated his supposed victory with his minions as his foe, the now-dead Son of God, lay lifeless in a small tomb. Satan thought he had won because he had seen Jesus breathe His last breath as He hung from that wooden cross. Little did Satan know that Jesus knew something he didn't; God had a plan and Jesus followed that plan to the end, and beyond.

On that Sunday, when He arose from the tomb, Jesus claimed the ultimate victory, victory over death itself. When He arose from the tomb, more alive than ever before, Jesus proclaimed to all who would listen that death no longer held its power over those who would believe. No longer was death the ultimate end; Jesus proved that eternal life was the reward for all who would follow His teaching and believe His words.

In our case, each of us must claim our personal victory. Only by surrendering will we know true victory, the same victory that Jesus received, victory over death. When it comes to our salvation, we receive our reward when we stop fighting God and surrender to Him and His will. We no longer have to fight; Jesus has fought our battle and won our victory. For us, that is truly a day to be celebrated.

Lord Jesus. I celebrate the fact that You have fought my battle, a battle that I could not win. I thank You for that victory and the reward awaiting in my heavenly home. Amen.

> *God is not a man, that He should lie, nor a son of man, that He should repent. Has He spoken, and will He not do it? Or has He spoken, and will He not make it good?* (Numbers 23:19)

LIMITED EXPECTATIONS

Charles Dickens, the English writer and social critic, wrote many stories about many things. He is considered by many to be the greatest novelist of the Victorian era. Living in the 19th century, Dickens' works included many of the things he encountered on a daily basis. Although his story, *A Christmas Carol*, is considered one of the greatest novels ever written, have you ever considered what expectations Mr. Dickens had as he sat down in 1843 and penned these words: "Marley was dead; to begin with"? It's amazing how a classical work of literature can begin with such an inauspicious collection of words.

If you can find a copy of the original book, you will find Mr. Dickens' expectations for his story in the preface. According to his own words, Dickens hoped his readers would not be, ". . . out of humor with themselves, with each other, with the season, or with me. May it haunt their houses pleasantly, and no one wish to lay it down." Dickens' expectation was limited to hoping people liked the story enough that they would actually finish reading it. Since movies didn't exist until the late 1800's, Dickens could not have envisioned the impact his little ghost story continues to have on the entire world now, more than a century after he died.

The third chapter of Acts tells a story of a lame man with limited expectations. Every day, his friends would carry him to the Temple gate so he could beg for money, hoping he would receive a few coins or perhaps a bit of bread from the passersby. He had no idea that before that day was over, his life would drastically change when he asked Peter and John for a bit of help. What he expected was a few coins and what he received was something he had never before been able to do. The man who was carried to the Temple that morning walked home that afternoon.

Do we limit God by our expectations when we approach Him in

prayer? Why do we so often ask for the minimum when we could just as well "shoot the moon"? While we shouldn't ask for worldly goods, we also mustn't limit God by asking Him for things we can accomplish, if only we apply ourselves and exercise those gifts He has given us.

Another classic work of Dickens is *Great Expectations*. Are our expectations of God merely good or are they great? Because we serve a great God, we should expect great things.

Heavenly Father. I pray I would not limit You with my requests. I pray You will show me the things I am able to do when I combine the wisdom and other gifts You have given me. And I pray I will apply that wisdom to know those things that are better left for You. Amen.

> *I will instruct you and teach you in the way you should go; I will counsel you with my eye on you.* (Psalm 32:8)

LEAVE THAT ALONE!

According to the Clemson University Cooperative Extension Program, eastern poison ivy (Toxicodendron radicans) is a woody, perennial vine or small shrub that can be found in fields, pastures, woodlands, farms, and home landscapes. Reading further, I learn that the entire plant is poisonous. Knowing this now, there was a time in my life that my response to that information would have been, "So?"

Being raised in the South, I spent many of my youthful hours roaming through woods, pastures, and fields that were flush with this plant of the devil. I can even remember a time in my life that I could, without wearing any gloves or other protective clothing, touch, accidentally or not, this plant and not be bothered by its irritating rash and itch. Even though I had been warned, "Leaves of three, let it be," I didn't worry about it. It didn't bother me. That all changed sometime in my twenty-third year.

While my sensitivity to urushiol, the plant's oil that causes the irritating reaction, is not terrible, my granddaughter, Lyra, is not so fortunate. Whenever I take her and Josh, her brother, for a walk, I make sure to point out any poison ivy so she will be spared the awful itching brought on by, in her case, the slightest brush of those dark green leaves. While we're at it, I also point out yellow jacket holes, fire ant beds, blackberry and rose bush thorns, unseen holes, and anything else I think might produce some pain in their lives. Why do I do this? Three reasons. One, while I realize pain is a part of life, because I'm their Poppa, I don't want them to get hurt. Two, I want each of them to be alert to those things in life that, if not paid attention to, can cause such pain. After all, the best treatment for an ant bite is not to get bitten. And three, because I love them.

Throughout our childhood, our parents would alert us to the hidden dangers that could be found in our daily walk. Leave that alone! Put that down! Pick that up! Don't touch that! Watch where you're going! From poison ivy to hot stove eyes to looking both ways before we crossed the street to poisonous snakes to running with scissors, to swallowing bubble gum (seven years is a long time), people who cared about us have constantly warned about things that, if given an opportunity, would jump up and bite us. Regardless of those warnings, inevitably, those things found a way to do their harm. Why? Either we sometimes let our guard down and lost our bearings, or worse, we recognized the danger and chose to ignore it, thinking we were too good to be bitten; that we were somehow in control.

For the Christian, sin is that thing that is waiting to bite us. Lying, stealing, cheating, lust, coveting, pride, using God's name in vain, these, and many more sins seem to be everywhere in our modern lives. Just about the time we avoid one temptation, we turn around and, if we're on the alert, we spy another one lurking just to the side of the beaten path, waiting for an opportunity to strike. And we can't say we weren't warned. First Peter 5:8-9 tells us the devil – our enemy – is a lion on the prowl, waiting for an opportunity to pounce on us when we least expect the attack. While the burn of a hand contacting a hot stove eye can be very painful, it is nothing compared to the cost that sin imparts on our eternal soul. Yes, the hot stove eye can cause a serious burn, but Romans 6:23 tells us that that the cost of sin is death.

Just as poison ivy and fire ants seem to be everywhere when we take a relaxing walk through the woods, temptation is practically everywhere we turn in our Christian walk. And just as we parents tried to warn our children of hidden traps and dangers, if we're a Christian, God has sent His Holy Spirit to guide us – His children – around the pitfalls that Satan has hidden especially for us, often where we least expect them to be. If we truly want to have less spiritual pain in our lives, when we hear God's Spirit tell us, "Leave that alone!", "Don't do that!", "Don't look at that!", or "Put that away!", we had best do what we are told.

Father God. I thank You for the gift that is my daughter. I also thank You for the two gifts that are my grandchildren. I ask that You direct my words and actions when I am with them, so they will not only recognize poison ivy and other physical dangers but will be able to recognize the dangers of temptation and sin lying in wait during their spiritual walk. Amen.

Acknowledgments

Whew! I finally finished book number two. I was wondering if I would ever get to that final period but somehow, it's done. With God's help and input, I've managed to put together another one hundred twenty-two stories about finding Him in the everyday. Anyway, it's time to get to the hard part. Whom to thank.

Well, to start off, I would be remiss if I didn't thank my mother. If it weren't for you, none of this would be necessary. For whatever reason, you put up with a rambunctious young man who sometimes didn't want to do what he was told. You could have given up, but, with God's help and your guidance, I've made it this far. I love you, Momma.

Now for Pop. You took one look at our somewhat dysfunctional family and, for reasons unknown to me, you thought that you would fit right in. You didn't have to do what you did, but you did, and I'm better for it.

Punkin. If someone had told me thirty-seven years ago how much happiness you would bring into my life, I wouldn't have believed them. I am overwhelmed with joy every time I remember that you are my daughter. Thank you for being the perfect daughter for me. I know you're married to Josh but, as the song says, I loved you first.

Lyra and Little Josh. You two bring a smile to my heart every time I hear you shout, "Poppa!" Mind your momma better than I did mine because, one of these days, you'll discover that she knows what she's talking about.

I could try to mention all the friends who have left footprints on my heart throughout my life, but I know I would omit more than I could name. Scattered throughout these pages are my memories of a life that we have shared during our limited time together. Some of you have been a part of my life from my earliest memories, and, despite all of the crazy things we did, we somehow made it this far. And for those few people who are my "longer than I care to name" friends, I wouldn't be near the man I am if it weren't for each of you. I couldn't imagine my life without each of you in it, so I won't.

To those men I share Wednesday nights with as we study God's Word, I thank you guys for the open and honest conversations we have sitting around those two tables. As I am, your families are blessed to have you in their lives.

To the leadership of First Baptist Church of Tuscaloosa, thank you for a wonderful church home.

Miss Sammie, thank you for your help and the encouragement with my work. When I told you I didn't have a book in me, you simply said, "Give it a try." Little did I know . . .

Ellen (a.k.a., My Book Putter Together Lady), thank you for your patience and your guidance during my first attempt at becoming a published author. I know I may be jumping the gun, but I appreciate what you will do with this one, book number two. I'm planning on using the same system we came up with before: you talk and I listen; it seemed to work then and it probably will again. I guess we'll find out if I learned anything from our initial venture.

Sunny and Gracie, I apologize for all the hours you two have laid at my feet, under my computer desk, and sometimes in my lap as I typed, waiting for me to give you a little bit of attention. Don't worry, both of you made the book.

And before I close, I want to thank the one and only Son of the Most High God. Why You did what You did for me is beyond my ability to comprehend, but I will be eternally grateful for that Easter morning nearly two thousand years ago when You rose from the tomb, providing a life for us that none deserve but is available to all who will accept. I humbly thank You.

Finally, because I don't like saying goodbye (if you're wondering why, that's a story in the first book), I won't say it here. I'll sign off from this book the same way I end all of my visits: "See y'all later."

Author's Bio

Randy Glover lives near Tuscaloosa, Alabama with his two dogs, Sunny and Gracie. He enjoys life, writing, photography, his family and friends, being a granddad (a.k.a. Poppa), fishing, and teaching children about God and Jesus at First Baptist Church of Tuscaloosa.

Made in the USA
Columbia, SC
17 November 2024

46242236R00154